GREAT ATHLETES
of the 20th century

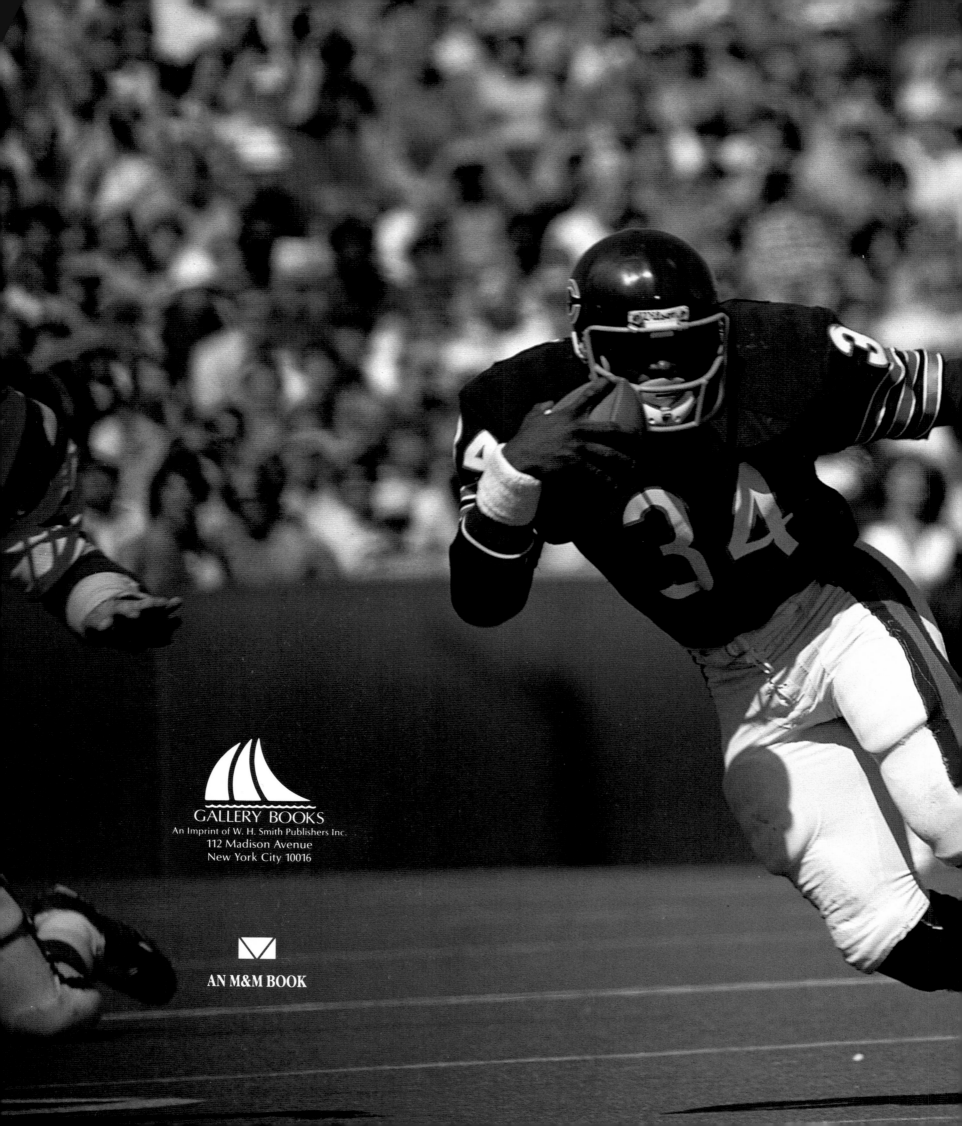

GALLERY BOOKS
An Imprint of W. H. Smith Publishers Inc.
112 Madison Avenue
New York City 10016

AN M&M BOOK

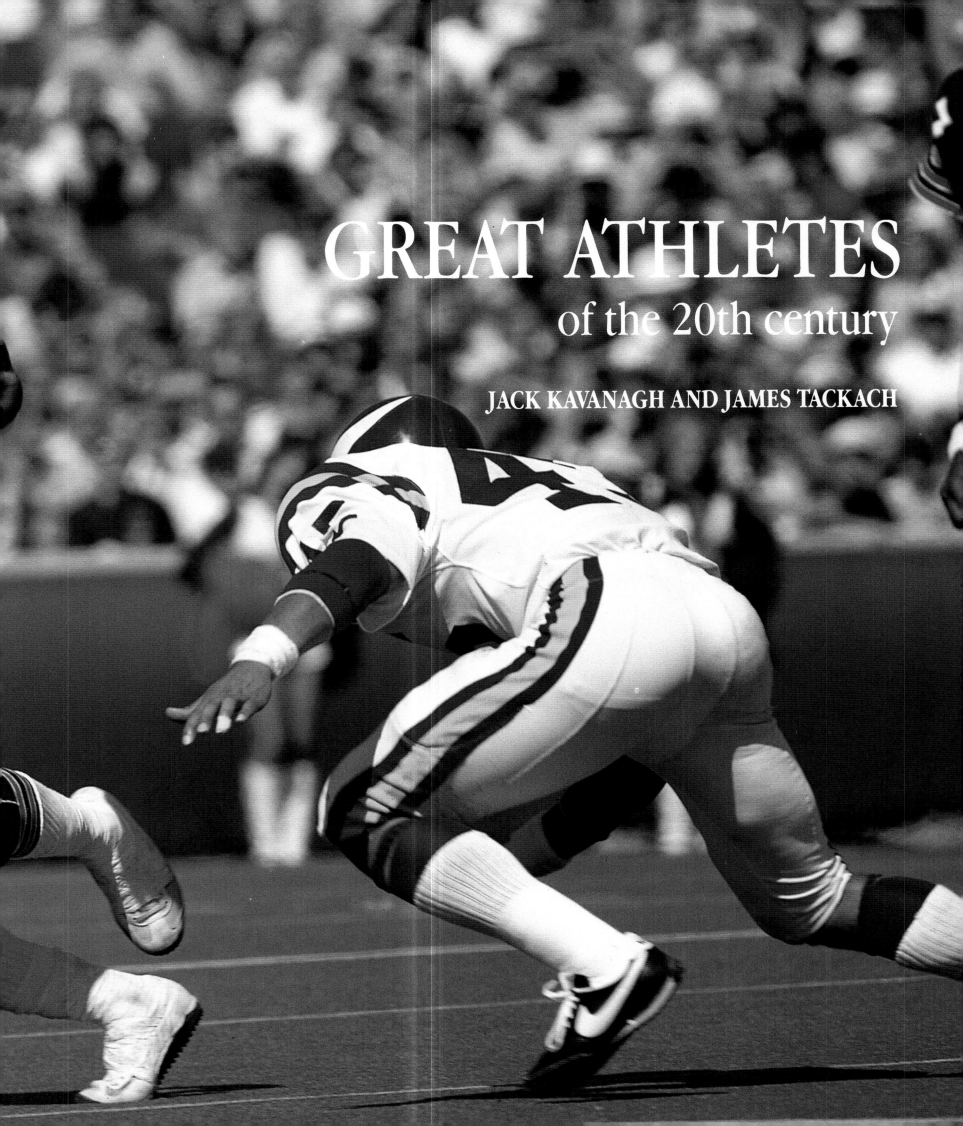

GREAT ATHLETES
of the 20th century

JACK KAVANAGH AND JAMES TACKACH

(Preceding pages) *Tough, agile, unafraid of contact, Walter Payton amassed a record 16,193 yards—an average of 4.4 yards a carry—in his 12 seasons with the Bears.* (See pages 102–103)

GALLERY BOOKS
An Imprint of W. H. Smith Publishers Inc.
112 Madison Avenue
New York City 10016

AN M & M BOOK

Copyright©1989 by Moore & Moore Publishing

ISBN 0 8317 3962 2

Great Athletes of the 20th Century was prepared and produced by Moore & Moore Publishing, 11 W. 19th Street, New York, N.Y. 10011

Project Director & Editor Gary Fishgall

Photo Research Jana Marcus, Ben McLaughlin, Lucinda Stellini

Senior Editorial Assistant Shirley Vierheller; **Editorial Assistants** Lisa Pike, Ben McLaughlin; **Editorial Assistance** Burt N. Zelman of Publishers Workshop, Inc.

Designer Binns & Lubin / Martin Lubin

Separations and Printing Tien Wah Press (PTE) Ltd., Singapore

Typesetting Sharon Brant Typography

This edition published in 1989 by Gallery Books, an imprint of W.H. Smith Publishers, Inc., 112 Madison Avenue, New York 10016

First published in the United States

CONTENTS

INTRODUCTION   7

BASEBALL   8

BASKETBALL   38

BOXING   62

FOOTBALL   82

GOLF   116

HOCKEY   134

OLYMPICS   148

TENNIS   166

INDEX   190

CREDITS   192

Introduction

The athletes we celebrate in this collection share one evident characteristic: they have all achieved greatness by the strictest of standards. Are they the *greatest* athletes of the century? Not necessarily, although unarguably some of them—like Babe Ruth, Muhammad Ali, Babe Didrikson Zaharias, Jim Thorpe, and Jack Nicklaus—would merit that distinction. What they all represent, without equivocation, is magnificent achievement in a chosen endeavor.

To define true athletic greatness is difficult because it rests, in part, on intangibles. Surely it begins with some special mix of outstanding physical attributes, hard work, and proper training, combined with mental discipline and an absolute will to win.

Surely, too, greatness implies excellence over a long period of time. Great athletes sometimes have an off-season or suffer an injury, but these setbacks are temporary. In fact, the ability to overcome setbacks and obstacles—be they early failure, frequent physical pain, or racial prejudice—is one characteristic that most of these athletes share.

Greatness also manifests itself in superb performance in the most crucial of tests: the World Series, the Super Bowl, the Olympics, a world championship fight, the U.S. Open. But true greatness does not need the crucible of a great event to shine. The athletes we revere have a spark, a charisma, that draws the crowd regardless of the importance of the

occasion. Small boys were taken to see Babe Ruth play even on a day when the Yankees were meeting a second-division team. People paid to see Jack Dempsey or Joe Louis work out with sparring partners in a gym. Devotees followed Bobby Jones or Arnold Palmer during practice rounds.

Moreover, the athletes we celebrate here are marked by a verve that goes beyond statistical measurement. They have performed in their sport with a grace and style obvious to even the most casual observers. Those who saw Joe DiMaggio patrolling centerfield, Julius Erving going to the basket, or Sonja Henie floating across the ice knew that they were seeing something special.

Of course, numerous athletes not included in this collection might also be listed among the great. But the decision to name only 100 individuals imposed certain limitations. We could not simply name 100 athletes irrespective of sport. We also had to resist the temptation to concentrate mostly on renowned athletes from the first half of the century at the expense of equally outstanding recent performers, although it is natural to dwell on those who have passed into legend. Furthermore, we have focused on women athletes as well as men, athletes of diverse origins, figures from abroad as well as Americans, amateurs and professionals—an appropriate cross section of the world sporting scene.

So, what follows is *our* selection of 100 stellar athletes. We hope you will find some old favorites and perhaps some less familiar names as well. If we inspire you to find out more about the sports figures presented here, so much the better. You may well be induced to compile your own list of greats as well. If so, you will no doubt find a wide range of superstars to meet your standard of excellence within the challenging world of 20th-century athletics.

(Opposite) *Babe Didrikson Zaharias, considered by many to be the greatest female athlete of the century, practices the hurdles in anticipation of the 1932 Olympics.* (See pages 134–135.)

BASEBALL

HENRY AARON

ACTIVE YEARS 1954–1976

HIGHLIGHTS* MVP (1957), home run leader (1957, 1963, 1967), batting leader (1956, 1959), RBI leader (1957, 1960, 1963, 1966), hit 755 lifetime home runs (first on all-time major-league list), drove in 2,297 runs (first on all-time major-league list); *Baseball Hall of Fame* (1982)

*National League

(Preceding pages) *It wasn't power. It was concentration and an intense will to win that led Pete Rose to break Ty Cobb's record of 4,191 hits.* (See page 31.)

Henry Aaron played superbly for more than two decades, but he will always be remembered for the moment in 1974 when he broke Babe Ruth's lifetime record of 714 home runs.

The man who broke Babe Ruth's lifetime home run record excelled at every phase of the game. He logged fourteen .300 seasons, played rightfield splendidly, and stole bases too.

That man, Henry Aaron from Mobile, Alabama, did not take long to establish himself as a player of extraordinary skill. In 1955, at age 21, he batted .314, hit 27 home runs, and knocked in 106 runs for the Milwaukee Braves. A year later, he won his first batting title.

The Braves of the mid-1950s were a solid team, and Hammerin' Hank helped them win a pennant in 1957, earning MVP honors for himself in the process. During the World Series, in which the Braves bested the Yankees, Aaron batted .393 and hit three home runs. A year later, the Braves again took the pennant, and in the ensuing World Series, Aaron batted an impressive .333—but this time in a losing cause.

During the 1960s, the Braves faded from contention and the team moved to Atlanta, but Aaron continued to excel at the plate and in the field. When he again tasted postseason play in the 1969 National League Championship Series, he whacked three homers in three games against a fine New York Met pitching staff.

He remained productive throughtout his career. Even at age 37 in 1971 he had a banner season: a .327 average, a career high of 47 home runs, and 118 RBIs. That season he hit his 600th career homer. By then, most baseball fans knew that Babe's lifetime mark of 714 home runs would eventually fall.

The date was April 8, 1974, and it came before a national television audience in Atlanta on a pitch thrown by the Dodgers' Al Downing: home run number 715! Aaron reacted to the hoopla and media attention with the same grace, dignity, and professionalism that marked his entire career.

Hank Aaron carved his place in baseball history with more than two decades of outstanding play. His lifetime total of 755 home runs might never be topped. As another slugger, Reggie Jackson, once put it, "If you hit 35 a year for 20 years, you're still 55 short."

GROVER CLEVELAND ALEXANDER

ACTIVE YEARS 1911–1930

HIGHLIGHTS* 373 winning games (tied with Christy Mathewson for most victories), holds 20th-century record for complete games (346) and total shutouts (90), twice won two games in a single day; *Baseball Hall of Fame* (1938)

N amed for one president and portrayed in the movies by another (Ronald Reagan in *The Winning Team*), Grover Cleveland Alexander combined heroism on the baseball field with debilitations caused by illness and alcoholism.

The raw-boned, 6-foot farm boy from Nebraska started in 1911 with the Philadelphia Phillies. In seven seasons with the club, he won 190 games, 30 or more in each of three successive years. In 1917 he was sold to Chicago, but World War I intervened. Serving as an artillery gunner in France, he came to the Windy City deafened by shell fire and suffering from epilepsy.

*National League

He remained baseball's best pitcher, but the raucous Prohibition town of Chicago aggravated his drinking problem and he was released by the Cubs midway through the 1926 season. He was picked up by the St. Louis Cardinals, a team he led to the World Series against the Yankees. The dramatic peak of Alex's life came in the seventh inning of the final game of that series when he was brought in to stop a New York rally with two out and the bases loaded. He did what was asked of him—he struck out the batter—and then held New York hitless during the last two innings.

He had one more good season, 1927; then the trail wound down. By 1930, Alex was washed up in baseball and drifted into an alcoholic's life, ending up in the dusty Nebraska towns of his youth where he died at age 62.

In his seven seasons with the Phillies, Grover Cleveland Alexander won 190 games, including 30 in each of three successive seasons.

YOGI BERRA

ACTIVE YEARS 1946–1963, 1965

HIGHLIGHTS* MVP (1951, 1954, 1955), played in 14 All-Star Games (more than any other major league catcher), holds several lifetime World Series records (games, at bats, hits, doubles), managed pennant winners in both major leagues (1964, 1972); *Baseball Hall of Fame* (1972)

T oday's baseball fans know Yogi Berra as the author of outrageous baseball sayings like "It ain't over 'til it's over." Baseball fans of the 1940s and 1950s, however, know Lawrence Berra, the strange-looking man from St. Louis' Italian ghetto, as the catcher and backbone of the Yankee teams that won 14 pennants and ten World Series in 17 seasons.

*American League

One of the best catchers of the 1950s, Yogi Berra is best known today for outrageous baseball sayings like "It ain't over 'til it's over."

He was one of the best receivers of his day, once catching a record 148 straight games without an error. He was a capable handler of pitchers too. On an October afternoon in 1956, Yogi coaxed nine perfect innings from a journeyman pitcher named Don Larsen—the only no-hitter in World Series history.

He was also a feared lefthanded hitter. Five 100-RBI seasons attest to his ability to hit in the clutch. He rarely struck out and built a reputation as a dangerous hitter who could connect on a pitch in or out of the strike zone.

In World Series play, Berra excelled. His dozen Series homers rank third behind the career totals of Mickey Mantle and Babe Ruth, and his individual Series batting averages are among the best.

After his long playing career, the three-time MVP continued in baseball, managing pennant-winning Yankee and Met teams and coaching pennant winners in New York and Houston.

ROGER CLEMENS

ACTIVE YEARS 1984–

HIGHLIGHTS MVP (1986), Cy Young Award winner (1986, 1987), ERA leader (1986), strikeout leader (1988)

Baseball managers love power pitchers—the fellows who throw three fastballs past opposing batters nine or ten times per game. Given a choice of any pitcher in the major leagues, most of today's managers would probably take Roger Clemens of the Boston Red Sox, the dominant power pitcher of the 1980s.

*American League

Strangely enough, Clemens, who was born in Dayton, Ohio, in 1962 and pitched high school ball in the Houston area, was ignored by major college scouts because they rated his fastball mediocre. So he ended up at San Jacinto Junior College, where he grew 4 inches and cranked up his fastball to 90 miles per hour. Then he received a scholarship to the University of Texas. By the time he pitched the Longhorns to victory in the 1983 College World Series, the major-league scouts were gathering in force.

He signed with the Bosox in 1983 and moved rapidly through the farm system, impressing onlookers with both his speed and his pinpoint control. In May 1984, he reached the majors and won 9 of his first 13 decisions, including a game in which he struck out 15 batters and walked none.

But an arm injury in 1984 and a shoulder injury the following season interrupted Clemens' development. In 1985, he pitched in only 15 games.

Before the 1986 season, the "Rocket Man" worked hard to get his right arm and shoulder in shape, and he opened the year with 14 straight victories. In one game, a 3–1 win over Seattle at Fenway Park on April 29, he struck out a record 20 batters. He kept winning and finished the season at 24–4, then won the deciding game of the American League Championship Series by pitching seven strong innings even though he was weakened by flu. He also looked like a winner in game six of the World Series against the New York Mets when he left after seven innings with a 3–2 lead, but the Sox relievers and defense blew the game in the 10th inning. Still, Clemens came away from the season with MVP and Cy Young honors.

In 1987, although Clemens did not quite match his phenomenal 1986 per-

Roger Clemens puts his entire 225 pounds behind this pitch, a fastball that few batters would like to face.

formance, he still won 20 games, including seven shutouts, and another Cy Young Award. In 1988, a midseason back injury prevented him from reaching the 20-game plateau, but he finished 18–12, led the league in strikeouts, and helped Boston win a divisional title.

The 6-foot 4-inch, 225-pound Clemens is an intimidating force on the pitcher's mound. Around the league, batters fear that they will be facing his fireballs for many seasons to come.

In his short career, Clemens has already won two Cy Young Awards and set a new single-game strikeout record.

TY COBB

ACTIVE YEARS 1905–1928

HIGHLIGHTS* batting champion (1907–1915, 1917–1919), highest lifetime batting average (.367), Triple Crown winner (1909), three times exceeded .400, leader in steals six times, second highest hit total (4,191); *Baseball Hall of Fame* (Charter Member—1936)

*American League

(Opposite) *Tyrus Raymond Cobb at the peak of his form in 1914. He played for Detroit in all but two of his 24 major-league years and managed the club for six seasons.*

(Below) *Cobb's artful fallaway style—and the spikes that he sharpened under the watchful eyes of his opponents—helped him lead the league six times in steals.*

Tyrus Raymond Cobb's greatness, as it appears in the cold type of the record books, was the result of his hot-blooded will to win. For 24 years, the 6-foot, 1-inch Georgian threw his 175 sinewy pounds into battle in every game he played.

The 4,191 base hits he lashed left-handed gave him an incredible 12 batting titles, nine of them in a row. Challengers drove him to new heights. When, for example, the rookie Joe Jackson hit .408 in 1911, Cobb hit .420, his highest average in a 24-season career.

Yet, to type the "Georgia Peach" by his batting skills is to miss the full dimension of the man. He was a better than average outfielder and his throws were always on the mark. Moreover, he was an awesome base runner. To his blazing speed he added intimidation, honing his spikes with a file in view of the other team. He also had quickness, surprise, and an artful fallaway style. And he was daring. In recent years, his season and career totals have been eclipsed, yet even Lou Brock, who stole more bases, never tried to steal home as Cobb did, not once or twice, but 50 times, with the final theft coming at age 41!

While his slashing style of play was admired, he was never adored. Not by the fans of Detroit, where he spent all but two seasons (he ended his career with the Philadelphia Athletics), nor by his teammates, most of whom loathed him. The furies that drove him to greatness followed him off the playing field as well. He fought under the stands; in hotel rooms behind locked doors—even with a teammate who had the temerity to use the tub before Cobb got there. "I've got to be first at everything," he explained, flooring his roomie with a punch.

During his many years in baseball, Cobb's connections outside the game made him a millionaire. He profited from early tips on motor stocks in Detroit and earned a tidy sum by investing in Coca Cola at the insistence of its Atlanta developers.

JOE DiMAGGIO

ACTIVE YEARS 1936–1942, 1946–1951

HIGHLIGHTS* MVP (1939, 1941, 1947), home run leader (1937, 1948), RBI leader (1941, 1948), batting leader (1939, 1940); *Baseball Hall of Fame* (1955)

I n the opinion of many, he was the quintessential baseball player of his era. Other players have had higher lifetime marks than Joltin' Joe, but few players have played the game with more grace and style.

Joe DiMaggio broke into the majors with the New York Yankees in 1936, and the 21-year-old rookie from San Francisco looked as if he had been playing big-league ball for a decade. He batted .323 that year with 29 homers and 125 RBIs. The next season he did even better, leading the league with 46 homers and driving in 167 runs.

But perhaps the high point of this remarkable career came in 1941, the second of his three MVP seasons, when DiMaggio hit safely in a record 56 straight games. The streak, which began on May 15, lasted until July 17, when Ken Keltner, the Cleveland third baseman, made two fine plays to keep DiMaggio hitless. Joltin' Joe bounced right back, however, hitting safely in 16 more consecutive games. The great streak should have surprised no one; in 1933, as a minor leaguer, DiMaggio had hit safely in 61 straight games.

Impressive too was Joe's performance in a late-June series against the second-place Red Sox in 1949. DiMaggio was making his first appearance of the season following a heel injury. In the first game, Joe singled and homered. In the second, he homered twice to turn a 7–1 Bosox lead into a 9–7 Yankee win. In the third, he hit a three-run homer to help the Yanks sweep the series. In short, after an eight-month absence from baseball, he batted .455, hit four home runs, and drove in nine runs in three games.

*American League

In addition to his power at the plate, DiMaggio displayed considerable defensive skill, gliding across centerfield in Yankee Stadium with the grace of a clipper ship, hence his nickname "The Yankee Clipper." Though he did not steal bases, he ran them well. In fact, his contemporaries maintain that he didn't make a single baserunning blunder during his entire career.

The husband of Marilyn Monroe, symbol of strength and fortitude in Ernest Hemingway's *The Old Man and the Sea,* and the epitome of bygone heroism in Simon and Garfunkle's "Mrs. Robinson," the Yankee Clipper has become a legend in his own time. It's a distinction Joe DiMaggio has earned.

Joe DiMaggio, who became the idol of little boys everywhere, receives the congratulations of his own son after the Yankees beat the Dodgers in the 1949 World Series.

(Opposite) Joltin' Joe twice led the league in batting, home runs, and RBIs and was elected MVP three times.

LOU GEHRIG

ACTIVE YEARS 1923-1939

HIGHLIGHTS* played 2,130 games, MVP (1927, 1936), Triple Crown winner (1934), home run champ (1931, 1934, 1936), first to hit four successive home runs in a single game; *Baseball Hall of Fame* (Special Election—1939)

I took a rare neurological illness to derail the "Iron Horse." Now called Lou Gehrig's disease, it wastes muscles and eventually kills its victims. In 1939, when it struck down the man who personified durability, it ended Gehrig's appearance in an incredible 2,130 consecutive games.

Henry Louis Gehrig was a New Yorker. He came to the Yankees from Columbia University. Once he was in the lineup as a regular, he never left it. He forms a link in the Yankee tradition that reaches from the glorious Babe Ruth era to the rise of Joe DiMaggio. But, unlike other Yankee greats over the years, Gehrig never pressed for individual honors. His satisfaction came from the team championships—the seven World Series—in which he participated. In these post-season games (34 altogether), he hit 10 home runs and batted .361, an impressive record that might have been even greater but for the times that the Yankees swept the Series in four straight.

Gehrig was a superb athlete. He excelled at football in college and was a far-ranging, sure-handed first baseman, throwing, as he batted, left-handed. He was a daring base runner when a base was needed; he stole home 15 times. He is remembered for his 493 home runs, but he led his league in triples and doubles, stats which show speed plus power. Perhaps most importantly, his ringing hits came with men on base. In fact, he holds the record for grand slams with 23 and is third in career RBIs with 1,990. Only Henry Aaron, who played in

*American League

(Opposite) *Lou Gehrig in the fourth game of the 1936 World Series. That year the "Iron Horse" led the league in home runs and in slugging.*

Despite the many honors that came his way, Gehrig remained a modest man whose primary satisfaction came from helping the Yankees win.

1,134 more games, and Babe Ruth, who was in 339 more, had greater RBI totals.

Lou Gehrig's single best season, 1934, disappointed the Yankee captain. He won the Triple Crown, with his only batting championship, .363, but New York failed to win the pennant. Two years later, in 1936, he led the league in home runs and in slugging average and started the Yankees on a run of four straight championships.

The last of these years, 1939, saw Lou as a nonplaying captain. Each day, more weakly, he carried the starting lineup—his name no longer in it—to home plate. On July 4th they held Lou Gehrig Day at Yankee Stadium, and a nation wept while the wasted Gehrig assured everyone, "Today, I consider myself the luckiest man on the face of the earth." Two years later they laid him to rest.

ROGERS HORNSBY

ACTIVE YEARS 1919–1937

HIGHLIGHTS* batting champion (1920–1925, 1928), second highest career average (.358), MVP (1925, 1929), Triple Crown winner (1922, 1925), manager, World Champion St. Louis Cardinals (1926); *Baseball Hall of Fame* (1942)

I n 1926 Rogers Hornsby was the toast of St. Louis. He had averaged over .400 from 1921 to 1925 and capped that achievement by managing the Cardinals to their first World Championship. But the handsome man they called Rajah was majestically aloof and high-handed. He owned stock in the team and wanted a three-year contract.

Instead, the owner, Sam Breadon, still simmering over a clash with his manager (who was sometimes known as Mr. Blunt), traded Hornsby to the New York Giants. It was a trade of contentious second basemen. Frank Frisch, who was in Giant manager John McGraw's doghouse, went to St. Louis and soon became the local favorite Hornsby had been.

Meanwhile, Hornsby continued along the baseball trail: one year in New York; a single season in Boston, where as player-manager he won his seventh, and final, batting title; and finally to Chicago, where he helped the Cubs to a pennant in 1929. A year later he was named manager. But he was fired late in 1932 by another offended management. That season the trailing Cubs went on to win the pennant, but the players coldly cut Hornsby out of the World Series profits.

Hornsby lived by his own standards. Next to baseball he most enjoyed betting on horses. When called to task for his avocation by Baseball Commissioner Landis, a foe of gambling, the Rajah insisted on his right to bet his own money. Thereafter Landis let Hornsby cut his own swath during his remaining years in baseball.

In 1926, player-coach Rogers Hornsby brought the Cardinals their first World Championship, only to be traded in what the New York Times *called "the biggest deal in modern baseball history."*

*National League

REGGIE JACKSON

ACTIVE YEARS 1967–1987

HIGHLIGHTS* MVP (1973), home run leader (1973, 1975, 1980, 1982), RBI leader (1973), hit 563 lifetime home runs

R eggie Jackson did everything in a big way. When he hit a home run, it traveled a great distance. When he struck out, he did so with a vicious swing. When he signed a contract, it was for big money. When he feuded with a teammate or manager, it made the front page.

The Pennsylvania-born Jackson began his career with the Oakland A's. In 1968, his first full season, he hit 29 homers, and the following year he pounded out 47 more. Soon, with Reggie in the line-up, the team developed into baseball's best, winning a divisional title in 1971, followed by three straight World Series

victories. During those championship seasons, Jackson became the most feared slugger in the league.

In December 1976, as a free agent, he signed a $3 million contract with the Yankees. He feuded with captain Thurman Munson and manager Billy Martin, but he averaged nearly 30 homers a year for five Yankee seasons, helping the Bronx Bombers to four divisional titles, three American League pennants, and two World Series championships.

He is probably best remembered for his postseason play. In five World Series, "Mr. October," as he is rightfully called, recorded a batting average of .357 and a slugging average of .755. Perhaps the highlight of his career came in the 1977 Series in which he batted .450 and hit five homers, including three on consecutive swings in the final game.

Jackson ended his career with 563 homers. No doubt when he becomes eligible for the Hall of Fame, his plaque will hang in Cooperstown.

*American League

A postseason batting average of .357 and a slugging average of .775 helped Reggie Jackson earn the nickname "Mr. October."

SANDY KOUFAX

ACTIVE YEARS 1955–1966

HIGHLIGHTS* MVP (1963), Cy Young Award (1963, 1965, 1966), ERA leader (1962–1966), strikeout leader (1961, 1962, 1965, 1966), leader in victories (1963, 1965, 1966), four no-hit games in four consecutive seasons (1962–1965); *Baseball Hall of Fame* (1972)

W hen Brooklyn-born Sandy Koufax broke in with his hometown Dodgers in 1955, he was a strong southpaw thrower who could not find home plate. Through his first six seasons, he averaged at least one strikeout per inning (18 in a game in 1959), but he walked too many batters to win consistently. After six seasons, he had amassed a pitching record of only 36 wins and 40 losses.

Suddenly, in 1961, Koufax's career took an abrupt turnaround. He reduced the number of walks and began to pitch more consistently. The result was his

*National League

first big season: an 18–13 record and a league-leading 269 strikeouts in 255 innings.

Koufax could always throw hard. Opposing batters claimed that his fastball looked like a white blur that rose sharply as it approached home plate. When he also learned to throw his sharp-breaking curve for strikes, he became the league's best pitcher. From 1961 through 1966, his final season, Koufax dominated his league as few pitchers have ever done. During these years, he won 129 games and lost only 47. He led the National League in strikeouts and shutouts four times, won the league ERA title five times, pitched four no-hitters, and won three Cy Young Awards.

With Koufax as their pitching ace, the Dodgers won pennants in 1963, 1965, and 1966. In each of those seasons, he won at least 25 games. He was also a major factor in postseason play. In the opening game of the 1963 World Series, for example, he fanned a record 15 Yankees. Then, in game four, he beat

Whitey Ford 2–1 to complete a Dodger sweep. In the 1965 Series, he won twice again. Working with only two days' rest in game seven, he shut out the Twins on three hits. In his career, Koufax worked eight World Series games and pitched to an ERA of 0.95.

Troubled by an arthritic throwing arm, Koufax retired after the 1966 season, having just won his third Cy Young Award. Many Hall of Fame pitchers have recorded more victories than his 165; most have thrown more innings and struck out more batters. But few pitchers have dominated baseball as Koufax did during the last six seasons of his career.

Sandy Koufax in action in the deciding game of the 1965 World Series in which the Dodgers beat the Twins, 2–0.

MICKEY MANTLE

ACTIVE YEARS 1951–1968

HIGHLIGHTS* MVP (1956, 1957, 1962), home run leader (1955, 1956, 1958, 1960), RBI leader (1956), batting leader (1956), Triple Crown winner (1956), 536 lifetime home runs, World Series record for home runs, runs, RBIs, walks; *Baseball Hall of Fame* (1974)

M ickey Mantle, a strong country boy from Spavinaw, Oklahoma, inherited the centerfield job at Yankee Stadium from the great Joe DiMaggio in 1952, the year after Joltin' Joe retired. It soon became apparent that neither life in the big city nor the DiMaggio legend could intimidate the new 21-year-old Yankee centerfielder.

He was a rare combination of awesome power and blazing speed who was once clocked running from the lefthand batter's box to first base in a sizzling 3.1 seconds. With this sprinter's speed, Mantle could patrol centerfield as widely as DiMaggio and could bunt his way out of slumps. But at 5 feet 11½ inches and 195 pounds, he could also hit tape-measure home runs. One of his enormous homers, hit in Washington, traveled 565 feet; another just missed being the first fair ball to leave Yankee Stadium. If Mantle were not constantly nagged by leg injuries, his career achievements might have been even greater. In the opinion of Yankee management, his postgame activities, especially his beer bouts with teammates Whitey Ford and Billy Martin, hurt his performance too. Still, the switch-hitting Mantle won three MVP Awards, led his league in homers four times, and is one of only eight American League players to win the Triple Crown.

Furthermore, during Mantle's Yankee years, his teams won 12 pennants, enabling him to set World Series records for homers, runs, RBIs, and walks. In

*American League

(Opposite) *While he was best known as a slugger, Mickey Mantle's blazing speed also helped him make effective use of the bunt.*

1964 he broke Babe Ruth's lifetime World Series home run record with a ninth-inning blast that took game three from the St. Louis Cardinals. Mantle also ranks second to teammate Yogi Berra for World Series games played, at bats, and hits.

A generation of baseball fans grew up with Mickey Mantle as their hero. His number 7, retired by the Yankees, still

adorns the uniforms of schoolboy Mantle worshipers. And even today, when a strong, young hitter with good legs breaks into the major leagues, someone invariably calls him the "next Mickey Mantle." But there's only one Mick, and there will never be another.

Mantle receives the congratulations of his teammates after a grand slam home run in the 1953 World Series.

ROGER MARIS

ACTIVE YEARS 1957–1968

HIGHLIGHTS* MVP (1960, 1961), home run leader (1961), RBI leader (1960–61), record holder for home runs in a single season (61)

Many fans think that Roger Maris's baseball career began and ended in 1961, when he erased Babe Ruth's single-season home run record. Actually, Maris played 12 solid major-league seasons, won two MVP Awards, and played in seven World Series with the New York Yankees and the St. Louis Cardinals.

Maris played his first three big-league seasons for mediocre teams in Cleveland and Kansas City. Yankee scouts, however, liked the young outfielder from Fargo, North Dakota, because his left-handed swing seemed perfectly suited to Yankee Stadium's short rightfield seats. So the Yanks acquired Maris after the 1959 season.

He immediately made the trade look good, hitting two homers, a double, and single in the first game of the 1960 season. He won MVP honors that year with 39 homers and a league-leading 112 RBIs. The next summer, he etched his name into baseball's record book.

Six weeks into the 1961 season, no one would have dreamed that Maris, with only three homers to his credit, would be chasing Ruth's home run record. But in the next 68 games, he hit 37 more, and the chase was on.

The pressure was almost unbearable. Reporters hounded Maris after every game, and many fans booed him because

*American League

Roger Maris hitting his 61st home run on the last day of the 1961 season to break Babe Ruth's record.

they wanted Ruth's record to stand, or because they wanted Maris's teammate, Mickey Mantle, to break the record. Baseball Commissioner Ford Frick added to the pressure by announcing that Maris would have to tie or break Ruth's record in 154 games, the length of the season in Babe's day, not in the 162 games that Maris would be playing. Maris lost tufts of hair, but he continued hitting homers.

In game 154, Maris hit his 59th homer, leaving Ruth a share of the record. The 60th came a week later, and the record 61st came on October 1, the final day of the season. For his achievement in 1961, Maris won another MVP Award.

During his seven seasons in the Bronx, the Yanks won five pennants. In 1967, after injuries had slowed him, he was traded to St. Louis, where he helped the Cards win two pennants and a World Series before retiring after the 1968 season.

Maris was a complete player who mastered every aspect of his game. Besides hitting homers, he ran the bases smartly and fielded brilliantly. Still, the baseball world has never fully acknowledged his fine career, or his great achievement in the summer of 1961. In 1984, the year before he died, the Yankees tried to atone for years of neglect by retiring his number and erecting a plaque at Yankee Stadium "in belated recognition of one of baseball's greatest achievements ever."

WILLIE MAYS

ACTIVE YEARS 1951–1952, 1954–1973

HIGHLIGHTS * Rookie of the Year (1951),
MVP (1954, 1965), home run leader (1955,
1962, 1964, 1965), batting leader (1954), stolen
base leader (1956–1959), 660 lifetime home
runs (third on all-time major-league list);
Baseball Hall of Fame (1979)

W illie Mays was one of those
special talents who comes
along once or twice in a
generation. With a rare combination of
power, speed, and hustle, he played
splendid baseball for more than 20 years,
finishing among the all-time top-10
players for games played, at bats, hits,
homers, runs, RBIs, and slugging.

An Alabama native, Mays came to the
big leagues at age 19 to play for the 1951
New York Giants. Mays helped the Giants
win the pennant that season and won
the Rookie of the Year Award himself.
He missed most of the next two seasons
while serving in the military, but he
returned in 1954 to win his first MVP
Award and to lead the Giants to the
World Series.

Perhaps Mays will be remembered
best for a defensive play in that 1954
Series, a catch that is still considered the
best in World Series history. It came in
the first game at the Polo Grounds with
Cleveland's Vic Wertz at the plate and
the score tied 2–2 in the eighth inning.
Wertz hit a 440-foot drive to deep
centerfield, and Mays, sprinting with his
back toward home plate, gloved the ball
for the inning-ending out. Cleveland
never recovered; the Giants won the
game in 10 innings and swept the next
three games of the Series.

*National League

Through the mid-1950s, Mays shared
the headlines with two other great New
York centerfielders, Mickey Mantle of
the Yankees and Duke Snider of the
Brooklyn Dodgers. When their careers
were over, Mays had the best record.

The Giants moved to San Francisco in
1958, and many Mays fans maintain that
the strong winds at Candlestick Park
hurt his lifetime hitting statistics. But he
still won three home run titles in San
Francisco, and in 1969 he became the
first National Leaguer to hit 600 lifetime
homers.

In 1972, the Mets acquired Mays in a
trade, and he played his final two seasons
in New York. His many fans were pleased
to have the "Say Hey Kid" back in town
once again.

Mays's Hall of Fame plaque states that
he "excelled in all phases of the game."
No one would dispute that statement.
He batted .302, hit 660 home runs, won
12 Gold Gloves for fielding excellence,
and played the game with an unmatched
intensity.

*Willie Mays had a special combination of
power, speed, and hustle. He was a superb
batter and base runner and was arguably the
best centerfielder of his day.*

*(Following page) The Say Hey Kid, who joined
the Giants when they played in Manhattan's
Polo Grounds, ended his career back in New
York with the Mets.*

25

STAN MUSIAL

ACTIVE YEARS 1941–1963

HIGHLIGHTS* batting champion (1943, 1946–1948, 1950–1952), MVP (1943, 1946, 1948), played in 24 All-Star Games and four World Series, batted 3,630 hits for a .331 average including 475 home runs and 1,951 RBIs; *Baseball Hall of Fame* (1969)

S tan Musial, a skinny six-foot Polish kid who came from the slag-heap town of Donora in western Pennsylvania, began as a left-handed pitcher. A sore arm in the low minors sent him to the outfield where his hitting rocketed him through the St. Louis Cardinal farm system to the big leagues.

Musial batted out of a left-handed crouch that uncorked a whiplash swing. This unique "peek-a-boo" stance, plus his durability and his legendary batting eye, brought him more than 50 big-league records during his 22-season career. He was first called "Stan the Man" by grudging fans at Ebbets Field who were awed by his hitting feats against the Dodgers. Apparently being away from St. Louis's Sportsman's Park didn't bother him. Of his 3,630 career hits, half—an unusually high total—were earned on the road. He was balanced in his field appearances, too. He is the only player in major-league history to have played more than 1,000 games in both the outfield and at first base.

*National League

Despite his skill and accomplishments, Musial was a modest man, a considerate team player who was easy to manage and always in shape to play. Off the field, he was a family man, who became a grandfather while still an active player. He was also part owner of a popular restaurant in St. Louis, the only city for which he played baseball and the place he made home.

When his time on the ball field ended, Musial moved into the Cardinal front office. Today he is senior vice-president and a member of the board of directors. He didn't want to be a field manager, although he brushed aside the assumption that he was too nice for the job. "Just the opposite", he said, "I'd be like other great players who tried to manage. They make everyone miserable, including themselves, trying to get others to play the way they did."

(Following page) *Musial's unique "peek-a-boo" stance helped him earn seven National League batting championships.*

Stan Musial shortly after joining the Cardinals in 1948. St. Louis was the only city in which he played during his entire 22 season major-league career.

SATCHEL PAIGE

ACTIVE YEARS 1922–1965

HIGHLIGHTS pitched as many as 153 games in one year, pitched more than 100 no-hitters, won 100 games with only 6 losses in 3 years, pitched 3 games the same day and won them all, pitched over 2,500 professional baseball gmes, winning over 2,000; *Baseball Hall of Fame* (1971)

By the time Leroy "Satchel" Paige reached the majors he was already a legend to the generations of baseball fans who had seen him dominate the Negro Leagues for decades. Still, when the Cleveland Indians signed Satchel in 1948, a year after Jackie Robinson broke baseball's color line, it was called a publicity stunt. The doubters said he was too old to pitch in the major leagues.

Indeed, Satchel's age was part of his mystique—he was always vague about it—but he had been pitching since 1922 and baseball people were sure the magic was gone from his right arm. It wasn't. After joining the Indians in mid-season, he won six critical games, including two shutouts and helped the Indians finish in a tie for first place. (In a one-game play-off, Cleveland beat Boston to take the pennant.)

It was a long road to Cleveland from the back-of-town part of Mobile, Alabama, where Leroy grew up. To earn money as a kid, he toted luggage at the train depot, tying the bags together and draping them around his gangling frame. To the other boys, he looked "like a satchel tree" and soon no one called him Leroy anymore.

In the early 1920s, Paige entered the loosely organized Negro Leagues. He also played on mixed teams in Latin America during the winters. Beginning about 1930, he barnstormed the country with his own touring team. Wherever he went, he was a star attraction who always lived up to expectations. He would sit his outfielders down and strike out the side. He would also pitch his curves, show his speed, convulse the fans with his "hesitation pitch," and then move on to the next town for the next payday.

Satchel had a flair for colorful statement. His explanation for longevity included the immortal, "Never look back, something may be gaining on you."

A special committee voted Satchel Paige into the Baseball Hall of Fame in 1971. Who knows what he might have accomplished had he joined the majors in his prime. Still, he's remembered for his showmanship, his homespun philosophy, and, above all, for his undeniable pitching skill.

By the time this photo was taken in the 1940s, Satchel Paige had been a star in the Negro Leagues for 20 years. In 1948, after Jackie Robinson desegregated baseball, Paige joined the Cleveland Indians.

JACKIE ROBINSON

ACTIVE YEARS 1947–1956

HIGHLIGHTS* Rookie of the Year (1947), batting champion (1949), MVP (1949), most stolen bases (1947, 1949), All-Star Game (1948–1954); *Baseball Hall of Fame* (1962)

A t age three, Jackie Robinson journeyed west with his mother and four older brothers and sisters after his father had deserted the brood back in Cairo, Georgia. His mother, who found work as a domestic in Pasadena, wrote home, "I'm living on the edge of heaven." Jackie found paradise, too, on the athletic fields of southern California.

In 1938, he entered UCLA, where he was a football All-American, lettering in four sports, baseball among them. In college he also met Rachel Isum, who became his wife and the mother of his four children.

During World War II, Robinson, a graduate of officer candidate school, had to serve in a segregated army. Although he had trouble reconciling his service to the "Land of the Free" while being relegated to the status of a second-class citizen, his experience in the war helped mold him into the man who would desegregate professional baseball.

In 1946, no black had ever played on a modern major league team, but Branch Rickey, general manager of the Brooklyn Dodgers, felt the time had come to change that. To do so, however, he needed a man who not only had the ability to perform on the field but one

*National League

with the strength of character to survive the abuse that he was sure to receive. Rickey felt Robinson, then a star for the Kansas City Monarchs, was that man.

On April 15, 1947, Jackie Roosevelt Robinson donned the Dodger blue and took the field against the Boston Braves. The color line in pro baseball was no more. But acceptance didn't come easily. Many a time the proud athlete silently stood the taunts from enemy dugouts and from hostile fans. In the process he earned the respect of his teammates. Though he was not highly visible in the civil rights movement, he used his access to government and business leaders to work for economic gains for blacks.

But, in his 10-year career, Robinson was more than a symbol. He was a star whose .311 career average, electrifying base running, and leadership earned him election to the Baseball Hall of Fame.

In 1956, he left baseball, already afflicted with diabetes, a disease which aged him prematurely. In 1972, at 53, he died.

(Top) *More than a symbol, Jackie Robinson was also a superb athlete with a career batting average of .311.*

(Above) *The sign's prohibition no longer applies to Robinson as he breaks major-league baseball's century-old color barrier, April 15, 1947.*

PETE ROSE

ACTIVE YEARS 1963–1986

HIGHLIGHTS* MVP (1973), batting champion (1968, 1969, 1973), Rookie of the Year (1963), All-Star Game (1965, 1967, 1969–1971, 1973–1982, 1984, 1985), most games played (3,371), most base hits (4,256), most at bats (13,411), hit in 44 consecutive games (1978)

T he whole character of Pete Rose is summed up in his nickname, "Charley Hustle." He hurried in a straight line, bowling over anyone who got in his way. But unlike Ty Cobb, whose record of 4,191 hits he broke, Rose did not play with a psychotic drive—only with a singleness of purpose. *(See photo, pages 8–9.)*

*National League

Pete Rose is a rarity in the limited geography of big-league baseball—a home town boy who made good. He was born in Cincinnati in 1941 and has made his home there all his life. Even in 1979, when a misguided management let him get away from the Reds, he only played baseball in Philadelphia. He lived in Cincinnati year-round. Then, after a brief stay in Montreal, a new ownership in Cincinnati brought him home as a player-manager.

It was on his own turf that he reached the zenith of his career. On the 57th anniversary of Ty Cobb's last major-league game, Pete Rose broke the "Georgia Peach's" record for most career hits. The event was expected once he closed in on Cobb's mark. The suspense was mostly about when and

where it would occur. In fact, it came on September 11, 1985, before a cheering hometown crowd.

As Pete Rose stood at first base, waving to the fans, he was joined by the batboy, his son Petey. It was an event to share with his family and his teammates—and with management. In appreciation, Reds' owner Marge Schott sent him home that night in a brand new red Corvette, already equipped with a license plate which read "4192"—Pete's new record.

Rose added 64 more hits to his total by the end of the next season, 1986. There, at 4,256, the record apparently rests, for since then Pete has remained a bench manager.

Breaking Cobb's record put pressure on Pete Rose, but he was no stranger to

producing under daily demands. In 1978, his pursuit of a consecutive game hitting streak became a daily story. Although he was stopped short of Joe DiMaggio's fabled 56 straight games, he tied the National League mark of 44, set in the last century by Wee Willie Keeler. During the streak he hit three home runs in one game, and in another, stole second, third, and home in the same inning.

There remains one goal for Pete Rose. He would like to manage the Reds to a pennant. It's the least a hometown Cincinnati boy can do.

Following his early home-town glory days with Cincinnati, Pete Rose contributed to the Phillies World Series victory in 1980. He returned to the Reds in 1984.

BABE RUTH

ACTIVE YEARS 1914–1935

HIGHLIGHTS* home run champion
(1918–1921, 1923, 1924, 1926–1931), batting
champion (1924), 60 home runs in a single
season (1927), 714 career home runs, highest
major-league slugging average (.690), most
major league walks (2,056), All-Star Game
(1933, 1934); *Baseball Hall of Fame*
(1936—Charter Member)

T o many people, Babe Ruth *is*
baseball. Although he has
been dead since 1948, he is
an unending source of wonder to all
who love the game.

In 1914, a crude 18-year-old from a
Baltimore industrial school was virtually paroled into baseball when George
Herman Ruth, son of a saloon keeper,
was turned over to Jack Dunn, owner of
the Orioles. The young 6-foot 2-inch
teenager, appropriately dubbed "Babe,"
soon developed into a promising pitcher
and, before the season ended, he was
sold to the Boston Red Sox.

In Boston he became the league's best
left-handed pitcher, winning 80 games
in five seasons. He also developed into a

*American League

powerful slugger, setting a new home run
record in 1919 with 29.

The 1920 sale of Babe Ruth to the
New York Yankees for $100,000 altered
the course of baseball history. The first
year he wore Yankee pinstripes, he hit
an unbelievable 54 home runs. Entire
teams did not hit as many. Because of
his hitting skill, he was shifted perma-
nently to the outfield and his promising
pitching career came to an end.

In 1923, Yankee Stadium, the "House
That Ruth Built," opened, and the Babe
filled it with fans. Three years later, in
1927, the "Sultan of Swat" reached

legendary heights when he hit what
seemed an unbreakable 60 home runs.
In the third game of the 1932 World
Series, he added to his legend by coming to bat in the fifth inning, taking two
strikes, pointing to a distant fence, and
then hitting the mark with the next
pitch. Or so the story goes.

In the waning years of his career, Babe
wanted to manage the team whose success he had created, but the Yankees
exiled him from the league. He was
picked up by the National League's
Boston Braves, who flimflammed him
with vague promises about the future.
Shortly after the start of the 1935 season,

a discouraged, flu-ridden Bambino
accepted the inevitable and retired.

When he was dying, the Yankees
invited him back for a last visit. In an
eloquent testimonial, his voice rasping
from the throat cancer that was killing
him, he spoke of the boys who had loved
him, saying that baseball belonged to
America's youth—not to the owners or
even the star players like himself. One
year later he was gone. Gone but not
forgotten.

*There will never be another like him. To many
people, Babe Ruth is baseball.*

(Opposite) *With over 700 home runs to his
credit, Babe Ruth made this sight a familiar
one to fans all over the world.*

With this 60th home run in 1927, Ruth established a single-season home run record that many thought would last forever but it was broken by Roger Maris 34 years later.

HONUS WAGNER

ACTIVE YEARS 1897–1917

HIGHLIGHTS * batting champion (1900, 1903, 1904, 1906, 1909, 1911), stolen base leader (1901, 1902, 1904, 1907, 1908), most career triples (252), 3,430 hits, 722 stolen bases; *Baseball Hall of Fame* (1936—Charter Member)

*National League

Born in 1874, as one of a western Pennsylvania miner's nine children, John Peter Wagner was destined for a life in the coal pits. Instead, the ungainly-looking man they affectionately called "Honus" became, in the words of his Hall of Fame plaque, "the greatest shortstop in baseball history."

Not only was he the best shortstop, he was also the National League's best hitter and base runner. His opposite number in the American League was Detroit's Ty Cobb, 12 years his junior. When they met in the 1909 World Series, the belligerent Cobb, prancing off first base, shouted, "Hey, Krauthead, I'm coming down on the first pitch." Making good his threat, Cobb tore into second and Wagner tagged him in the mouth. The Detroit hitter's lacerated lip was secondary to his ripped ego and he ended the Series, which Pittsburgh won in seven games, batting only .231. Wagner, by contrast, hit .333 and stole six bases to Ty's pair.

But Cobb aside, Honus Wagner was hard to stir to anger. He was a kindly man who didn't even argue with the umpires. One of the few things he protested has given him an odd immortality with contemporary baseball card collectors: Wagner, who despised smoking, refused to allow his card to be given away with cigarettes, despite the fee it would have earned him. The few cards that got out are now worth over $25,000 each.

Money was not very important to Wagner. Once he reached $10,000 with the Pirates, he'd sign a blank form each season and tell the owner, "same as last year is all right." Late in his life the old ball player needed a job and Pittsburgh made him a 60-year-old coach. He became a traveling ambassador in a Pirates uniform, giving hitting tips, telling droll stories and enjoying his celebrity. He coached until he was 71 and was a living legend until his death, 10 years later.

The Baseball Hall of Fame calls Honus Wagner "the greatest shortstop in baseball history." He was also the National League's best hitter and base runner.

TED WILLIAMS

ACTIVE YEARS 1939–1960

HIGHLIGHTS* batting champion (1941, 1942, 1947, 1948, 1957, 1958), home run leader (1941, 1942, 1947, 1949), MVP (1946, 1949), Triple Crown winner (1942, 1947), 2,019 career walks (second to Ruth), last to hit over .400 (.406 in 1941); *Baseball Hall of Fame* (1966)

A skinny, fresh, and confident teenager from San Diego reported to the Boston Red Sox training camp in 1938 and announced that he planned to become the greatest batter in baseball history.

His name was Theodore Samuel Williams and soon he made good on his boast, hitting .406 in his third season, 1941. While he was the last batter in baseball history to reach this level, the principal interest that season was on his rival, Joe DiMaggio, who hit safely in a record 56 consecutive games.

Off the field, the "Splendid Splinter" was somewhat impetuous. Only critical baseball writers kept him from being his own worst enemy—*they* were! Unable to fault his hitting, they ridiculed him for his exuberant, sometimes naive, insistence on individuality. He refused to wear a necktie, for example, fumed at pretense, and gave razzing fans the finger. He spat toward the press box and wouldn't tip his cap when he hit a home run.

During World War II, he served as a pilot in the Marines; when he returned to Boston in 1946, he led the Red Sox to the World Series. Six years later the Korean conflict saw reserve combat pilot Williams return to active duty. His plane crashed once in flames but he walked away.

In 1954, he was back to full-time baseball, but due to a fractured elbow in

*American League

On July 13, 1943, former Red Sox star Babe Ruth posed with current Red Sox star Ted Williams to the delight of the sports photographers.

the 1950 All-Star Game, a neck injury, and weak legs, he now played in pain. Despite these ailments, however, the 39-year-old Williams hit .388 in 1957 to lead the league. He also hit 38 home runs, knocking out three in a single game on two occasions. The next year, at 40, he led the league in batting again!

In 1959, an injury-impaired season kept him from hitting over .300 for the only time in 19 seasons, but he refused to retire. Instead, a healthy Williams left the game in 1960 as he wished to, hitting .316 and earning his 29th home run of the season on his final time at bat. When he circled the bases that last time, running out his 521st home run, he glanced up at the Fenway press box and, while he did not spit, he did not tip his cap either!

(Opposite) *In his rookie season, 1939, the 6-foot 3-inch, 160-pound Williams shows why he came to be called the "Splendid Splinter."*

BASKETBALL

KAREEM ABDUL-JABBAR

ACTIVE YEARS 1965–1989

HIGHLIGHTS All-American—UCLA (1967–1969), Rookie of the Year* (1970), All-Star First Team* (1971–1977, 1980, 1981, 1984, 1986), scoring leader* (1971, 1972), rebounding leader* (1976), MVP* (1971, 1972, 1974, 1976, 1977, 1980), record-holder for most seasons played,* games played,* points scored,* field goals attempted,* field goals made*

H e dominated basketball at every level. As Lew Alcindor, he owned the New York City high school courts. At UCLA, he won All-American honors three straight years. And as Kareem Abdul-Jabbar, he ruled the NBA, scoring more points and winning more MVP Awards than anyone who has ever played the game.

When he graduated from New York's Power Memorial High in 1965, the 18-year-old Alcindor was already 7 feet tall and the target of every college coach. He chose UCLA, and with Alcindor on the court, the Bruins captured three straight NCAA championships. At one point, they won 47 consecutive games.

In 1969, the Milwaukee Bucks, one of the worst teams in the NBA with a 27–55 record, drafted Alcindor, and he immediately made the team a winner. They finished at 56–26 in 1970 and

*National Basketball Association

lasted two rounds in the play-offs. The next year, with Alcindor averaging 31.7 points per game, they won the NBA title.

By this time, Alcindor had changed religions and names and had grown to 7 feet 2 inches—though many opponents claimed that he was 2 or 3 inches taller. He was the league's best center—a commanding rebounder, devastating shot blocker, and explosive shooter who could score from close to the basket with powerful slam dunks or from outside the key with his rafter-scraping skyhook.

But, in 1976, frustrated by failures in three straight play-offs, the Bucks traded Abdul-Jabbar to the Lakers. It took the Lakers five seasons to surround Kareem with a quality supporting cast, but when they did, the team became an NBA power-house, winning league championships in 1980, 1982, 1985, 1987, and 1988.

Those Laker teams were filled with stars—Bob McAdoo, Magic Johnson, James Worthy—but, in the crucial game or series, the Lakers always looked to Kareem for a big performance. In the final round of the play-offs against the Celtics in 1985, for example, Abdul-Jabbar's 30-point, 17-rebound performance in game two (after a disastrous first game in which he scored only 12 points and grabbed three rebounds) inspired the Lakers to a six-game victory and another NBA title.

As Abdul-Jabbar entered the 1988/89 season, his twentieth and final year as a player, he had 37,639 regular-season points and another 5,595 in play-off games, 8,000 more than his closest competitor. He will retire with a record that no player has matched.

(Preceding pages) *Known for his great drives to the basket, Jerry West moves in on the Bucks' Oscar Robertson to go for a two-pointer.* (see page 61.)

(Left) *In the 1987 NBA finals, two former UCLA greats, Kareem Abdul-Jabbar and Bill Walton, find themselves in opposition.*

(Above) *In 1980, Abdul-Jabbar won his sixth and final MVP title as the Lakers beat the Supersonics in the semi-finals, shown here.*

(Opposite) *Utilizing his inimitable skyhook, Abdul-Jabbar led the NBA in scoring twice and earned a total of 37,639 regular season points by the end of the 1987/88 season.*

ELGIN BAYLOR

ACTIVE YEARS 1955–1972

HIGHLIGHTS All-American—Seattle University (1958), NCAA tournament MVP (1958), 35th Anniversary All-Time Team* (1959–1965, 1967–1969), Rookie of the Year (1959), All-Star Game Co-MVP (1959); *Basketball Hall of Fame* (1976)

Elgin Baylor had a ready wit, was equally adept at defense and offense, and was an articulate supporter of the game he played so well.

Baylor's basketball talent took root in the city of Washington, where he was born in 1934, and flowered in the state of Washington, where he won All-American honors at Seattle University.

In 1958, he joined the Minneapolis Lakers as a first-round draft pick and was named Rookie of the Year. The following season, he established a new NBA single-game scoring mark with 64 points against the Celtics; in 1960, he broke his own record with 71 against the Knicks.

At 6 feet 5 inches and a muscular 225 pounds, Baylor was a gift to any coach. Not only was he a scoring marvel whose point average exceeded 35.0 for three years in a row, he was also outstanding defensively. As a rebounder, he instinctively found the key position in most situations and willingly fed the ball to teammates in order to maximize scoring opportunities.

In 1960, Baylor and the Lakers moved to Los Angeles, where he was soon joined by another superstar, Jerry West. Baylor, who played both the front and back courts, used his diverse talents wherever they suited the team's needs.

In the following season, U.S. Army reservist Baylor's career was interrupted when the Berlin Crisis forced his recall to active duty. As he did with most things, Baylor served agreeably.

In 1962, when he returned to the

*National Basketball Association

Lakers, he picked up where he left off, earning a 34.0 point average, the second highest in the league after Chamberlain. Over the next 10 years, Baylor established himself as the premier power forward in the game, helping the Lakers to the final round of the play-offs seven times, only to see his team lose the championship in each instance. While he never again broke 30 points for a seasonal average,

he maintained a respectable 25.4 or better through 1968 (except for 1965/66 when he fell below 17) and he was named to the All-Star First Team six times.

Plagued by knee injuries, Baylor retired before the end of the 1971/72 season. Ironically, the championship that had eluded him throughout his 14-year career came to the Lakers that May.

Despite a relatively poor showing during the regular season, Elgin Baylor displays his former brilliance in the 1966 play-offs.

LARRY BIRD

ACTIVE YEARS 1975–

HIGHLIGHTS* *The Sporting News* College Player of the Year (1979), All-American—Indiana State University (1978, 1979), MPV* (1984–1986), All-Star First Team (1980–1988), Rookie of the Year (1980), Play-off MVP (1984, 1986), All-Star Game MVP (1982)

T hey say you can take the man out of the town but you can't take the town out of the man. And perhaps no one exemplifies that aphorism more than Larry Bird, a farm boy from the heart of Indiana. In a state that has contributed a wealth of out-

*National Basketball Association

standing players, Bird is perhaps the best. To many he *is* Indiana basketball.

Born in 1956, young Larry was the star of his team in French Lick when Bobby Knight, coach at Indiana University, beckoned. But, after a year, Bird fled to the small-town atmosphere at Indiana State, hardly a basketball powerhouse, where he became America's most talented collegian, leading his team to the NCAA finals in his senior year.

In Boston, Red Auerbach, whose Celtic dynasty had gone into eclipse, coveted the forward so avidly that he drafted Bird as a junior, waiting an entire year for him to graduate before seeing him join the team.

When the "hick from French Lick" reached the big time of the NBA he proved reticent off the court and sensational on it. He was named Rookie of the Year and voted First Team All-Star, an NBA honor that he would receive for the next seven seasons. He also led the way to a divisional title in his first year and, in the next, helped return the Celtics to the top of the league. There the team would stay, earning eight divisional titles in Bird's first nine seasons and three NBA play-offs. A truly gifted all-around player, he excels on offense and defense, and what he lacks in speed, he makes up for in guile and court savvy.

Between NBA seasons he returns home to Indiana, dressing casually, investing locally, and enjoying the rough fellowship of friends from his Hoosier farm-boy years. They talk about basketball, the state's religion, filling Larry in on neophytes who have appeared on the high school scene. It's like telling a god who has it made that there are no new deities coming along to challenge him for his throne. There may never be.

During the 1986 NBA finals with the Houston Rockets, Larry Bird led the Celtics to their 16th championship and was named play-off MVP.

WILT CHAMBERLAIN

ACTIVE YEARS 1955–1973

HIGHLIGHTS All-American—University of Kansas (1958), Rookie of the Year* (1960), MPV* (1960, 1966, 1967, 1968), scoring leader* (1960–1966), rebounding leader* (1960–1963, 1966–1969, 1971–1973), assist leader* (1968), All-Defensive First Team* (1972, 1973), 31,419 career points (second on all-time list*); *Basketball Hall of Fame* (1978)

H e was the NBA's first giant. The 7-foot 1-inch Wilt Chamberlain entered the NBA in 1959, after an All-American career at the University of Kansas and a year with the Harlem Globetrotters, and the big men have dominated the game ever since.

Born in Philadelphia in 1936, Chamberlain broke into the NBA with his hometown Warriors and promptly led the league in scoring with a 37.6 average. Two seasons later, he set a single-season scoring mark with an astonishing 50.4 points per game, a record that is unlikely to be broken. That same season, on March 2, 1962, he scored 100 points in a game against the Knicks in Hershey, Pennsylvania. It is unlikely that that record will be broken either.

Wilt the Stilt was a man of enormous power. No player dared block his smashing two-handed dunks. His playing weight was listed at 275 pounds, but he was really close to 300, and all muscle. He once broke up a fight on the court by picking up one of the 6-foot 8-inch combatants and carrying him to a neutral corner.

*National Basketball Association

The one major frustration in this brilliant career was that Wilt's teams were repeatedly denied the NBA championship by the Bill Russell–led Boston Celtics. Only once, when the two great centers battled in the play-offs, did Wilt's team come out on top. That was in 1967, when Chamberlain's 76ers finished the regular season with a 68–13 record and swept through the play-offs, losing only four games, to win the NBA

title. Late in his career, Chamberlain was traded to the Los Angeles Lakers, but his team was twice beaten in the NBA finals by the Knicks.

Because of these bitter defeats, the 1971/72 season might stand out as Wilt's finest. That season, Chamberlain's Lakers—a team which included Jerry West, Gail Goodrich, and Happy Hairston—won a record 33 straight games at midseason, finished at 69–13, and swept through the play-offs to the NBA title

with only three losses. During those play-offs, Wilt averaged only 14.7 points per game—he concentrated on defense and rebounding late in his career—but was named the play-off MVP.

Today some NBA teams have two or three seven-footers. Chamberlain was the first of these giants—and probably the best.

Chamberlain leads the Lakers past the Knicks in 1972 for the team's first championship since it moved to Los Angeles.

(Opposite) *In 1987/88, Bird's foul-shot percentage was .916, the sixth highest in NBA history.*

(Left) *At 7 feet 1 inch and 275 pounds of sheer muscle, Chamberlain simply dominated the game during the 1960s. How many players could ever surround a basketball with one hand as he did?*

(Right) *The classic battles between Chamberlain and Russell came to an end in this 1969 championship series which marked Russell's final outing as a player.*

BOB COUSY

ACTIVE YEARS 1946–1963, 1970

HIGHLIGHTS All-American—Holy Cross (1950), Rookie of the Year* (1951), MVP* (1957), named to All-Star First Team 10 times, assist leader 8 times*; *Basketball Hall of Fame* (1970)

Bob Cousy, one of the game's all-time great ball-handlers, demonstrates his proficiency as he dribbles past Milwaukee's Bob Harrison on November 11, 1954.

Coach Red Auerbach, who has seen a lot of players run up and down a basketball court, called Bob Cousy "undoubtedly the best backcourt player" in basketball history. Perhaps old Red, who coached Cousy for so many seasons, is a bit prejudiced. Nonetheless, not many who played with or against Bob Cousy would disagree.

Ironically, Auerbach did not want Cousy when the youngster came to the Celtics in 1950. Bob, who was born in Queens in 1928, had been an All-

American at Holy Cross, but pro scouts considered the 6-foot 1-inch guard too small for the NBA. Auerbach got stuck with Cousy when the Chicago Stags folded before the 1950/51 season and the team's players were spread around the league. Philadelphia, New York, and Boston drew lots for the Stags' last three players, and the Celtics, to Auerbach's dismay, drew Cousy's name.

Old Red was never more mistaken. Cousy immediately became his play-maker, running the offense and passing with a precision never before seen. He passed behind his back, between his legs, and right through lunging defenders. He could score too. On March 23, 1953, he became the first NBA player to score 50 points in a play-off game—a quadruple overtime Celtic victory over the Syracuse Nats.

During his first few years with the Celtics, the team played well but not spectacularly. Then in 1956, Bill Russell arrived, and the Celtics, with Russell at center and Cousy at guard, dominated the NBA, winning six league championships. Boston fans credit the two men with inventing the famous Celtic fast break—a rebound by Russell, an outlet pass to Cousy, and a long downcourt pass to some other Celtic streaking to the basket.

Cousy retired in 1963 (he made a three-game comeback in 1970) after 13 Celtic seasons with almost 17,000 points and an 18.4 scoring average. In every season, he was named to the All-Star team. For many years, he made Red Auerbach a foolish but happy man.

*National Basketball Association

DAVE DeBUSSCHERE

ACTIVE YEARS 1959-1974

HIGHLIGHTS played in 7 NBA All-Star Games, NBA All-Defensive Team (1969-1974); *Basketball Hall of Fame* (1982)

Dave DeBusschere was a rare athlete who played two professional sports. He pitched for the Chicago White Sox in 1962 and 1963 (and retired with a 3–4 lifetime record) and played forward for the Detroit Pistons and New York Knicks from 1962 until 1974.

He was born in Detroit in 1940, attended high school in Detroit, played basketball at the University of Detroit, and was drafted on the first round by the Detroit Pistons in 1962. In his third NBA season, he also became the Pistons' coach.

Ironically, his career blossomed immediately after he left Motor City. On December 19, 1968, the Pistons traded their all-star forward to the Knicks for Howard Komives and Walt Bellamy. DeBusschere joined a Knick team that was developing into an NBA powerhouse, with Walt Frazier, the hot new star, and Dick Barnett, the steady veteran, at guards; Bill Bradley, the Rhodes Scholar at forward; and Willis Reed in the middle.

The coach of that Knicks team, Red Holzman, stressed team basketball, and DeBusschere fit right in. He played rugged defense, he passed to the open man, and though he was only 6 feet 6 inches he grabbed 10 rebounds per game. DeBusschere was just what the Knicks needed to take off. That season he helped the team to the play-offs and a first-round sweep of the high-scoring Baltimore Bullets. The Knicks lost in the second round to the Celtics, but better days were ahead.

During the 1969/70 season, the Knicks and DeBusschere played brilliantly. They won their division, swept through the early play-off rounds, then upended a talented Laker team in the NBA finals to give the Knicks their first NBA championship in 24 years. In the seventh game of that series, with Reed injured, the Knicks relied on big Dave to keep the Lakers off the boards. He pulled down 17 rebounds and scored 18 points. Three years later, the Knicks won another NBA title, again beating the Lakers in the finals.

DeBusschere, one of the NBA's most consistent players, retired after the 1974 season with a 16.1 scoring average. Basketball fans, particularly Knick fans, are happy that he gave up pitching.

Although he was best known as a rebounder, Dave DeBusschere could score as well and finished his career averaging over 16 points a game.

JULIUS ERVING

ACTIVE YEARS 1969-1987

HIGHLIGHTS ABA MVP (1974, 1975, 1976), NBA MVP (1981), played in 16 ABA and NBA All-Star Games in 16 seasons, ABA All-Defensive Team (1976), All-Star First Team (1978, 1980–1983), 30,026 career points (third on all-time list)

Julius Erving brought showtime to the NBA. Other players before him—Oscar Robertson, Elgin Baylor, Earl Monroe—were smooth and even acrobatic. But "Dr. J" repealed the law of gravity on NBA courts and, in the process, changed the game of basketball.

It took years for the basketball world to notice Dr. J. At Roosevelt High (Erving was born in Roosevelt, New York, in 1950), he was a solid but not spectacular 6-foot 3-inch guard. He played college ball at the University of Massachusetts, hardly a collegiate powerhouse. When he turned pro in 1971, he played for the Virginia Squires of the ABA, the league that could not get a television contract and that played with a strange red, white, and blue ball. Erving averaged almost 30 points per game in his first two ABA seasons, but no one was watching.

Fans first took notice during the 1976 ABA finals. The Doctor, playing then for the New York Nets, put on a show against the Denver Nuggets that re-defined basketball. In game one, Erving twisted, leaped, and jammed his way to 45 points—18 in the final 7:43—to give the Nets a 120–118 victory. In the next game, a loss for the Nets, Erving scored 48. He was "held" to 31, 34, 37, and 31 points in the next four games, but when the six-game series was over, he had scored 226 points, grabbed 85 rebounds, and earned a new championship ring.

The Nets entered the NBA in 1976 but foolishly sold Erving to the Philadelphia 76ers. Finally, the basketball world saw the Doctor perform regularly. For 11 seasons, he soared to the backboard, hung in the air while gravity briefly lost hold, and filled the basket with an assortment of unbelievable jams and jumpers. Others scored more points, but no one played the game more spectacularly than Erving.

The highlight of Erving's Philadelphia years came in 1983, when, after four final-round play-off losses, he finally played on an NBA champion. The 76ers breezed through the three play-off rounds with only one loss. The great center Moses Malone was the team leader, but with six seconds left in the title-clinching game against the Lakers, it was Erving's long jumper that iced the game.

Julius Erving retired in 1987 with over 30,000 career points and a reputation as one of the classiest players ever to wear a uniform. Today's NBA acrobats—Dominique Wilkens, Michael Jordan, Magic Johnson—owe a great debt to basketball's great professor, Dr. Julius Erving.

(Left) *In 1976, Julius Erving went to Phila-delphia where he played spectacular basket-ball for 11 seasons, leading his team to an NBA title in 1983.*

(Opposite) *The Nets' Dr. J took center stage during the 1976 ABA finals with 226 points and 85 rebounds in the six-game series.*

JOHN HAVLICEK

ACTIVE YEARS 1959–1978

HIGHLIGHTS* All-Star First Team (1971–1974), All-Defensive First Team (1972–1976), 26,395 career points (fifth on all-time list); *Basketball Hall of Fame* (1983)

John Havlicek filled the gap in the great Boston Celtic dynasty between Bob Cousy—who played his last season in 1962, Havlicek's rookie year—and Larry Bird, who arrived in 1979, two seasons after Havlicek retired. While Hondo wore Celtic green, the team won eight NBA championships.

The son of Czech immigrants, Havlicek was born in Ohio in 1940 and played basketball on the splendid Ohio State teams of the early 1960s. With Havlicek and Jerry Lucas, another future NBA all-pro, the Buckeyes won the NCAA title in 1960 and reached the NCAA finals the next two seasons. The Celtics made Hondo their first-round draft choice in 1962.

Some thought that he would be too small for the NBA. He played forward in college, but at only 6 feet 5 inches he might not fit that position in the NBA. Yet he was not judged a good enough ball handler to play guard. Nonetheless, Havlicek became both a guard and a for-ward, maybe the best swing man in NBA history. At forward, he hustled rebounds by getting good position, and he worked on his ball handling until he became an All-Star guard.

For his first several NBA seasons, Havlicek was primarily a sixth man who came off the bench in the middle of the first quarter to give his team a spark. But, even in that role, he averaged 35 minutes and 19 points per game. Later, when he became a starter, he averaged well over 20.

Above all, Hondo was known as a clutch player who made the big hoop or big steal with the game on the line. Perhaps his biggest play occurred in the seventh game of the 1965 play-off against

*National Basketball Association

Critics found the young John Havlicek's ball-handling skills wanting but great defensive players like the Knicks' Walt Frazier gave him good "on the job" training.

the Philadelphia 76ers. With five seconds left in the game and the Celts leading 110–109, the 76ers had to inbound the ball under their own basket. A single basket would have ended the Celtics' season. But, as Hal Greer made the in-bound pass, Hondo cut in front of Greer's target and stole the ball to pre-serve Boston's win. Celtic fans can still hear their radio announcer, Johnny Most, screaming over and over, "Havlicek stole the ball! Havlicek stole the ball!"

There were other big plays as well by the man who went 16 seasons on the NBA's best team. With John Havlicek on the court, the Celtic tradition was in very good hands.

MAGIC JOHNSON

ACTIVE YEARS 1977–

HIGHLIGHTS All-American—Michigan State (1979), Rookie of the Year* (1980), assists leader* (1983–1987), All-Star First Team* (1983–1988), MVP* (1987)

I n 1979, when Earvin "Magic" Johnson left Michigan State University after his sophomore year to play for the Los Angeles Lakers, many basketball fans thought that he

*National Basketball Association

had made a mistake. No one doubted his future potential—he had just led the Spartans to an NCAA title over Larry Bird's Indiana State team—but some thought that the 20-year-old kid who had spent his whole life in Lansing, Michigan, was not yet ready for the NBA. How wrong they were!

In his first NBA season, Magic averaged 18 points per game, played in the All-Star Game, won Rookie of the Year honors, and led the Lakers to an NBA title. He played the difficult position of

point guard with the smarts of a 10-year veteran and turned a slow team into a high-scoring, fast-breaking showstopper that ran opponents off the court.

In that season's NBA finals against Philadelphia, Magic showed his talent and versatility by playing point guard, shooting guard, power forward, small forward, and center. In the final game of the series, a 123–107 Laker win, Magic replaced the injured Kareem Abdul-Jabbar at center and played the game of

his life: 42 points, 15 rebounds, 7 assists. The kid who wasn't ready for the NBA walked off with the play-off MVP trophy.

By 1981, Johnson was the NBA's best guard—maybe its best all-around player. He was one of the league's highest percentage shooters and best passer, and at 6 feet 9 inches he could rebound like a power forward. Not surprisingly, in Magic's first nine seasons, the Lakers won five NBA championships.

Magic's best season was 1987. Asked by coach Pat Riley to provide more scoring, Johnson responded with an average of 23.9 points per game, five more than his lifetime average. And his passing did not suffer; he led the league in assists for the fifth straight season with a career-high 977. He sliced up the Celtics with his shooting and passing in the NBA finals and was voted the league's MVP.

Magic led the Lakers to a second straight NBA title in 1988. It was the first time in almost 20 years that a team won back-to-back championships. As Magic entered the 1988/89 season, his 10th, he was still playing with the enthusiasm and vigor of a rookie. This fine career is far from over.

With his customary grace, Magic Johnson helps the Lakes defeat the Celtics in the 1988 finals.

Everything must be going the Lakers' way as Magic flashes his famous smile from the bench.

GEORGE MIKAN

ACTIVE YEARS 1942–1956

HIGHLIGHTS All-American—DePaul University (1944–1946), All-Star First Team* (1949–1954) scoring leader* (1949, 1950–1952), championship teams* (1949, 1950, 1952–1954), NBL championship teams (1947, 1948), voted Best Basketball Player in First Half of Century by Associated Press (1950), 25th and 35th Anniversary All-Time Teams* (1970 and 1980); *Basketball Hall of Fame* (1959)

Born in suburban Chicago in 1924, George Mikan wanted to play New York's Carnegie Hall, not Madison Square Garden. As a boy he had studied at the Joliet Conservatory, but the concert world lost a 6-foot 10-inch pianist when the other kids ridiculed him. Instead of hunching over a keyboard he rose to heights of basketball greatness.

At 245 pounds, the big man became Ray Meyers' first protégé at DePaul University, learning to play center in a way that revolutionized basketball. Not only did he rack up point totals, becoming the collegiate scoring leader in 1945, he was, in the opinion of Knicks' coach, Joe Lapchick, "the best feeder out of the pivot the game ever had."

Of course, it was Mikan's scoring that the early NBA fans came to see. The spectacled giant would lumber down the floor, set up in the pivot, and hit hook shots with either hand or feed off to a cutter or an open man. The big man was a forceful rebounder too, leading the NBA in 1953.

*National Basketball Association

Championships followed wherever George Mikan played. After leading DePaul to a national college title in 1945, he led professional teams to championships in seven out of eight seasons. In 1954 he retired, at 30, to practice law, but he came back for one season a year later to help Minneapolis try to hold onto the Lakers' franchise. Mikan again retired, and, except for a term as commissioner of the ABA in 1968/69, maintained a thriving law practice in the Midwest.

George Mikan's status and success were largely determined by his size and style of play. His dominance brought the 24-second clock to the NBA and the game has evolved into one of quicker—and even bigger—men. However, Red Auerbach, general manager and coach of the Boston Celtics, said about Mikan, "That man would have been a standout anytime, anywhere and under any conditions."

George Mikan leaps high for a lay-up in the 1953 play-offs which Minneapolis took four games to one against the Knicks.

OSCAR ROBERTSON

ACTIVE YEARS 1957–1974

HIGHLIGHTS leading NCAA scorer, University of Cincinnati (1958–1960), All-American—University of Cincinnati (1958–1960), Olympic gold medal winner—basketball (1960), 35th Anniversary All-Time Team* (1980), MVP* (1964), All-Star First Team* (1961–1969), Second Team* (1970, 1971), Rookie of the Year* (1961), All-Star Game MVP* (1961, 1964, 1969), championship team, Milwaukee* (1971), leader in assists* (1961, 1962, 1964–1966, 1969), leader in free-throw percentage* (1964, 1968); *Basketball Hall of Fame* (1979)

L ike many great black athletes, Oscar Robertson was born in a Southern state but grew up in the North. The Robertsons migrated from Tennessee, where Oscar had been born in 1938, to seek work in Indianapolis during the Depression. Then, as now, Hoosiers followed basketball with a religious fervor and Oscar played the game like a native-born son. At Crispus Attucks High School, he led the team to the first undefeated season in the history of Indiana scholastic basketball.

They already called him the "Big O" when he arrived at the University of Cincinnati, a trolly-line school without a reputation as a basketball power. He was so dynamic on the court that fans immediately knew something special had arrived in the Queen City. He led the NCAA in scoring the three full seasons he played for the Bearcats and was named an All-American each year. In 1960, his days as an amateur ended in glory when the U.S. basketball team, of which he was co-captain, took the gold at the Rome Olympics.

*National Basketball Association

As might be expected, the Cincinnati Royals used its territorial choice to make its home-state star a first-round pick in 1960 and Robertson lived up to his potential, earning Rookie of the Year honors and a spot on the All-Star First Team, a place that he would earn for nine successive seasons.

Robertson was not only a brilliant individual player, he was also a superb team player, one who led the NBA in assists six times. His main goal was to bring a championship to Cincinnati, but his best years came at a time when the Boston Celtics dominated the league; it wasn't until 1971, when he was with the Milwaukee Bucks, that Robertson played on a championship team.

In 1973, two years after that championship season, Robertson retired. He wanted to leave the game before age and diminishing skills dimmed the luster of his outstanding capabilities. And, in that, as in everything else he did, he succeeded. In 1979, his first year of eligibility, he was elected to the Basketball Hall of Fame.

A determined Oscar Robertson goes for the basket in 1974, his final season in the NBA.

(Opposite) *The Big O's unique one-handed release helped him lead the league in free-throw percentages in 1964 and again in 1968.*

BILL RUSSELL

ACTIVE YEARS 1953–1969

HIGHLIGHTS NCAA championship—
University of San Francisco (1955, 1956),
Olympic gold medal winner—basketball
(1956), selected Greatest Player in History of
the NBA by basketball writers (1980), 25th and
35th Anniversary All-Time Teams* (1970,
1980), MVP* (1958, 1961–1963, 1965). All-Star
First Team* (1959, 1963, 1965), Second Team*
(1958, 1960–1962, 1964, 1966–1968), championship teams* (1957, 1959–1966, 1968,
1969); *Basketball Hall of Fame* (1974)

*National Basketball Association

Born in Louisiana in 1934, Bill Russell grew up—to 6 feet 10 inches—in Oakland, California. A gangling, uncoordinated boy, he only began to show promise at basketball as a high school senior and felt lucky to have a basketball scholarship from the University of San Francisco across the bay. Russell, emerging as a defensive standout, and extraordinary rebounder, led the Dons to back-to-back NCAA championships. An invitation to join the 1956 U.S. Olympic basketball team followed.

Returning from Melbourne with a gold medal in hand, Russell was ready to play professional basketball and let it be known that his services would come high. Ready to pay the price, Boston swapped two former All-Americans, Easy Ed McCauley and Cliff Hagan, for the St. Louis Hawks' draft pick in order to secure the center for the Celtics.

"Until Russell, no one in the NBA played defense," explained Red Auerbach, the Celtics' coaching genius. He convinced Russell the other team couldn't score if they didn't have the ball and Bill's role became that of grabbing rebounds and starting fast breaks. But Russell could also excel at offense using his inside skill for tip-ins. At his own end he intimidated the other team's offense, blocking shots and forcing bad ones.

When Wilt Chamberlain joined the league, Russell was the NBA's leading center. Unable to match Wilt the Stilt for height, he compensated with quickness. And, over the next 10 seasons, the legendary duels between these superstars often found Chamberlain, who could stuff the ball standing on his tiptoes, watching his shots slapped away by the agile Russell. The Celtics won 10 titles, seven in succession, with Russell at center. In the last two, he was also the team's coach, the first black man to attain a coaching spot in the NBA.

During the 1968 play-offs, Bill Russell was the guardian of the middle as his defense sparked the Celtics to victory in six games.

(Opposite) *Tommy Heinson and Woody Sauldsberry—6 feet 7 inches and 6 feet 6 inches, respectively—can only watch as the "big men," Bill Russell and Wilt Chamberlain, battle it out.*

A water-drenched Russell grins as the Celtics win the 1968 finals over the Lakers for Boston's eighth championship in nine years.

JERRY WEST

ACTIVE YEARS 1957–1974

HIGHLIGHTS All-American—West Virginia (1959, 1960), Olympic gold medal winner—basketball (1960), 35th Anniversary All-Time Team* (1980), All-Star First Team,* (1962–1967, 1970–1973), Second Team* (1968, 1969), Play-off MVP* (1969), single-season record holder in free throws* (1966), All-Star Game MVP* (1972); *Basketball Hall of Fame* (1979)

C abin Creek, West Virginia, like small towns everywhere, had one local boy who was the best player at every game. His name was Jerome Alan West. But, of all the games at which "Zeke from Cabin Creek" excelled, he loved basketball the most. That skill took him to places—and led him to accomplish things—that most small town fellows only contemplate. *(See photo, page 38–39.)*

Born in 1938, West chose to attend the state university in West Virginia. There he was twice selected as an All-American and, in 1959, voted outstanding player in the NCAA tournament. The following year he became a member of the U.S. basketball team that took the gold medal at the Rome Olympics. He returned home, a first-round draft pick of the Minneapolis Lakers, to join the team in 1961 in its new home, the Los Angeles Forum.

Thus began a 12-year search for the NBA championship. In addition to West, the Lakers featured two other all-time greats, Wilt Chamberlain and Elgin Baylor, but the play-off titles went to Boston and New York. Nevertheless, individual honors flowed to West. He was named to the NBA's All-Star First Team eight times, and the Second Team twice.

*National Basketball Association

With his eyes squarely on the basket, Jerry West displays the intense concentration that marked every game he played.

He was a dedicated team player and no one ever played with more emotion, particularly in the closing minutes when he often salvaged games at the final buzzer. West recklessly thrust his 6-foot 2-inch body into every court battle, his 180 pounds pummeled by the bigger men he guarded. His nose was repeatedly broken but, Jerry's shooting eye was always sharp.

It took 12 hard-fought NBA seasons for the Los Angeles Lakers to finally win the title in 1972. Jerry's shooting average that year was slightly lower than his career mark, but he led the league in assists for the first time. Always a team player, a superstar at both ends of the court, Jerry West had at last reached the pinnacle of his career.

In 1973/74 he was again selected for the All-Star First Team, but his many hard court battles had finally caught up with him and, at the end of that season, he retired. Three years later the Lakers made him their coach and, in 1977, he won the Pacific Division title. While NBA championships eluded the team during his three coaching seasons, he had still reached his goal as a player—a team championship to go along with his many individual honors.

(Opposite) *Russell scores in early action during the deciding game of the 1965 Eastern Divsion play-off.*

BOXING

MUHAMMAD ALI

ACTIVE YEARS 1960–1967, 1970–1981

HIGHLIGHTS Olympic gold medal—Light Heavyweight Division (1960), World Heavyweight Champion (1964–1967, 1974–1978, 1978–1980), a record of 56–6 (37 KOs)

He called himself "the greatest" and, in the opinion of many, he was. Born Cassius Clay, a poor Kentucky boy, he gained worldwide acclaim as Muhammad Ali, the name he adopted when he became a Muslim in 1965.

Ali entered the pro ranks in 1960, shortly after taking the Olympic gold medal in Rome. By 1964, he'd earned a shot at the heavyweight title then held by the powerful "Black Bear," Sonny Liston. "I'll take him in eight," Ali—an

8–1 underdog—predicted and on February 25, to the amazement of the sports world, he did, when Liston failed to answer the seventh round bell.

Over the next few years, the new champ ran up an impressive string of victories against the likes of Patterson, Terrell, and Folley. Then, in 1967 he was stripped of his title and barred from the ring for refusing military service on religious grounds. For almost four precious years, he sat idle while Jimmy Ellis and Joe Frazier succeeded him as champ. Then, finally, in 1970, as the Supreme Court reviewed his case (and ultimately overturned it), he was issued a license once more. Determined to regain his title, he fought contender after contender. Finally, on March 8, 1971, he met Frazier in a classic battle at Madison Square Garden but lost on points.

Three years passed but, on January 22, 1974, he avenged himself on "Smokin' Joe" in another brutal battle and, later

that year, took on Frazier's successor, George Forman, for the crown. It was October 30, 1974, and after seven rounds in which Ali let the much younger champ punch himself out (a strategy he called "rope a dope"), Ali scored an eighth round knockout. He was "the greatest" once more. And, to prove it, on October 1, 1975, he again met his nemesis, Joe Frazier. It was billed as the "Thrilla in Manilla" and it lived up to its name but, after 14 brutal rounds, Frazier failed to answer the bell, and Ali remained champ.

He retained his crown for another three and a half years, but age was catching up to him. Finally, on February 18, 1978, a poorly conditioned Ali lost to a young Leon Spinks. Everyone figured he was through, but he met Spinks again seven months later and

regained his title, becoming the first heavyweight in history to win the championship three times. Despite his victory, however, Ali was basically at the end of his amazing career and, after losses to Larry Holmes and Trevor Berbick, he retired.

His decline in later years should not blind us to his incredible skill in his prime. At 6 feet 3 inches and 212 pounds, he had the power of a heavyweight but the speed of a much lighter man. He could, as he put it, "float like a butterfly and sting like a bee." That skill plus his good looks and flamboyant personality made him unforgettable.

(Preceding pages) *On this knock-out blow to Jersey Joe Walcott's jaw, Marciano became heavyweight champion of the world, September 23, 1952.* (See pages 76–77.)

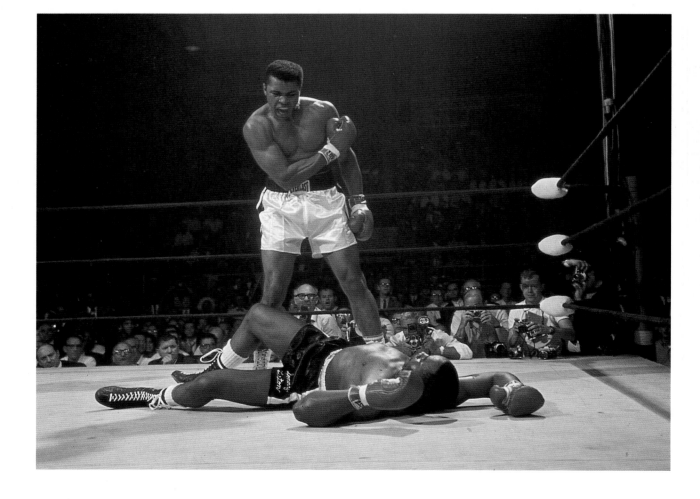

Muhammad Ali will not let up on Sonny Liston even after he's knocked him down in the first round of their rematch, September 25, 1965.

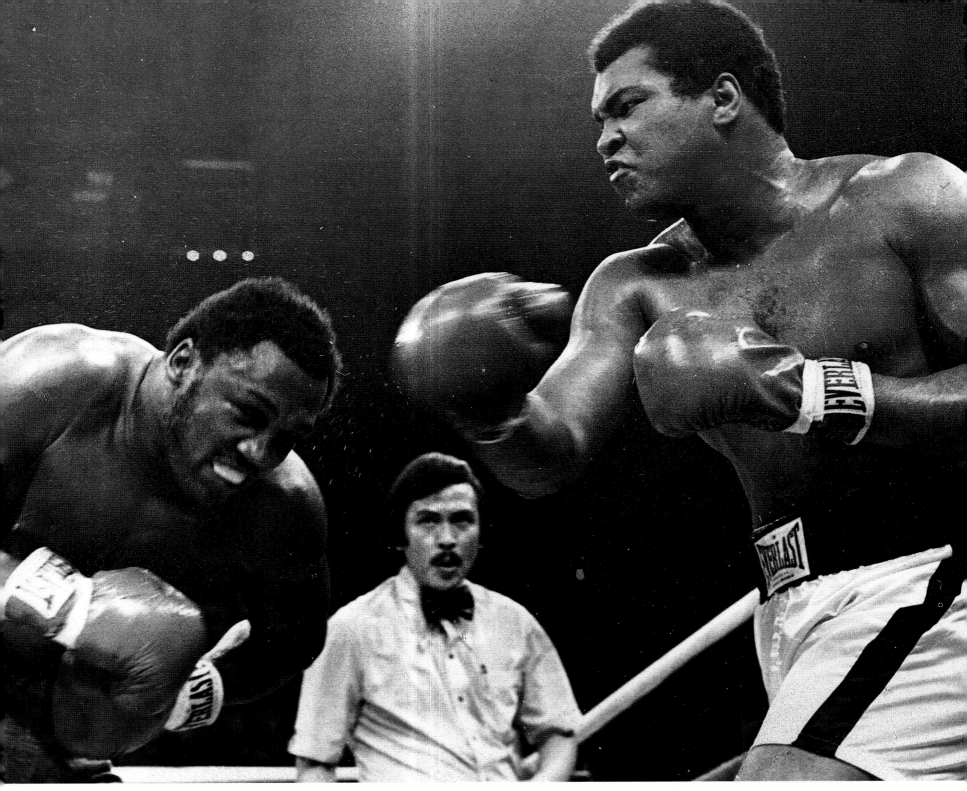

At the "Thrilla in Manilla" Ali and Joe Frazier pounded each other for 14 rounds, but, when all the fireworks were over, Ali was still champ.

(Following page) *Before his first meeting with Frazier, a confident Ali raises his hands in victory, but that night belonged to Smokin' Joe.*

JACK DEMPSEY

Jack Dempsey, the "Manassa Mauler," at his training camp, August 18, 1922.

ACTIVE YEARS 1915–1927

HIGHLIGHTS World Heavyweight Champion (1919–1926), a record of 62–6–10 (49 KOs)

Jack Dempsey, whose Colorado birthplace provided the name the "Manassa Mauler," was one of 11 children of an itinerant laborer. The son grew into a young hobo, taking fights where he could find them. He might never have been more than a wandering brawler had he not met wily manager Jack Kearns. The pair barnstormed the country, demolishing foes and taking aim at Jess Willard's heavyweight crown. The unsuspecting giant was lured into the ring in Toledo, Ohio, on July 4, 1919, and destroyed by Dempsey's ruthless attack.

At the time of Dempsey's win, America was embroiled in World War I. The new champ's failure to serve in the military aroused considerable ire, which Kearns deflected by casting Dempsey as the "American defender" in a 1921 title bout against Georges Carpentier of France. The fight produced boxing's first million dollar gate as Carpentier, a genuine war hero but barely a light heavyweight, lost to the champ in a fourth round KO.

In 1923, Dempsey met Luis Firpo in the most action-packed brawl ever fought. Dempsey floored the "Wild Bull of the Pampas" seven times in the first round alone. And, in between trips to the canvas, the challenger punched the champ out of the ring and into the ringside reporters, who shoved him back in, thus preventing a Dempsey knockout. Both fighters survived the first round pummeling, but Dempsey ended the carnage with an uppercut in the next round.

A long period of inactivity followed, primarily because there was no one to fight. Dempsey turned 30, married actress Estelle Taylor, and allowed the edge of competition to be dulled. Nevertheless when he was matched with Gene Tunney, an easy fight was expected. Instead, the ex-Marine easily outpointed Dempsey and took the title on September 23, 1926. In the following year's rematch, Tunney was knocked groggy in the seventh round. He rested on the canvas for 14 seconds, in what became known as the "long count," then outboxed the pursuing Dempsey to retain the title.

Defeat brought Dempsey lasting popularity. He made amends for his lack of military service by joining the Coast Guard during World War II and leading a landing party against the Japanese at Tarawa. For many years he was a partner in a leading New York City restaurant and died, in 1983, at 88.

On July 4, 1919, Dempsey defeated Willard to become the new heavyweight champ after this third-round knockout.

Dempsey, at 6 feet and 192 pounds, was 6 inches shorter and nearly 60 pounds lighter than Jess Willard.

Johnson on the canvas in the 26th round of his 1915 bout with Jess Willard. Was he knocked down or shielding his eyes from the harsh Havana sun?

Johnson flashes the grin that infuriated his opponents—in and out of the ring.

JACK JOHNSON

ACTIVE YEARS 1899–1915

HIGHLIGHTS World Heavyweight Champion (1908–1915), a record of 86-10-11 (40 KOs)

John Arthur Johnson, born in Galveston, Texas, in 1878, punched his way into the 20th century against any brawling opponent he could find, often fighting for $5 bills thrown on a barroom floor. Along the way, he took on the prejudices of his age to emerge as the first black heavyweight champion.

In the early 1900s, it was virtually impossible for a black contender to get a shot at the title in the United States. But the champ, Canadian Tommy Burns, agreed to battle Johnson on December 26, 1908, in Sydney, New South Wales, Australia. After 14 rounds in which Johnson pummeled the lighter man, the police stopped the fight, and the man they called the "Galveston Giant" was the new champion.

Johnson's strutting style, impudent grin, and white girlfriend (whom he later married, one of his two white wives) inflamed racial passions. The boxing community was desperate for a "White Hope." When none emerged, the former champ, Jim Jeffries, came out of retirement to do the deed. The two met in Reno, Nevada, on July 4, 1910. Johnson defeated the flabby Jeffries in the 15th round. In several Southern cities, celebrating blacks were assaulted in brutal race riots.

Johnson won more fights but, in 1912, he was convicted of violating the Mann Act for transporting a woman across a state line for immoral purposes and fled to Europe.

Meanwhile the hunt for a "White Hope" went on. Finally, Cowboy Jess Willard emerged. At 6 feet, 6½ inches and 240 pounds, he dwarfed even Johnson. He was also a genuine fighter and well trained. The champ, unable to enter the United States, agreed to fight in Havana. On April 15, 1915, in the 26th round, under a grueling sun, Johnson hit the canvas to end the bout. Some claim it wasn't a blow from Willard but the extreme heat that brought Johnson down. Either way, the heavyweight championship passed back into white hands. When it was recaptured by a black man, Joe Louis, 20 years later, race was a far less significant factor.

The ex-champ eked out an aimless life abroad until he ended his exile and served his sentence. After a year in prison, he opened a gym in New York's Harlem and survived on his celebrity. He died in 1946 in a car wreck in North Carolina. He was driving north from a circus engagement.

Jack Johnson poses for the camera in 1909, one year after becoming the first black heavyweight champion of the world.

RAY LEONARD

ACTIVE YEARS 1976–

HIGHLIGHTS Olympic gold medal—Light Welterweight Division (1976), held six different boxing titles throughout career (WBC Welterweight, WBA Junior Middleweight, WBA Welterweight, IBF Middleweight, WBC Super Middleweight, WBC Light Heavyweight), a record of 35–1 (24 KOs)

T he world first took notice of Ray Leonard, a 20-year-old kid from the Washington, D.C. area, when he breezed to a gold medal in the Montreal Olympics. On November 30, 1979, three years after turning pro, he beat Wilfred Benitez to win his first title, the WBC Welterwight crown.

Although he was named after Ray Charles and nicknamed after Sugar Ray Robinson, fight fans compared him to Muhammad Ali. Both were good-looking and articulate; both played to the crowd.

And like Ali, Sugar Ray was fast with his fists and footwork. He was a boxer, not a brawler.

But six months after beating Benitez, Leonard had his first setback. In a bout later called the "Brawl in Montreal," he lost a close but unanimous 15-round decision to tough Roberto Duran; on November 25, the two met again in New Orleans, and this time Leonard came out the victor. The fight was stopped in the eighth round when Duran, complaining of stomach cramps, shouted, "No maś, no maś!"

Two years later, after beating all the top fighters in his weight classes, Leonard suffered a detached retina in his left eye during a training session and retired, with a 32–1 record.

But the eye healed, and he began training again. His target was middleweight champ Marvin Hagler, the hardest puncher in the world and the owner of a 62–2–2 record with 52 knockouts. The boxing world thought Leonard was crazy.

The battle between Sugar Ray and Marvelous Marv took place on April 6, 1987, with a record $25 million at stake. The fight was close. Hagler stalked Leonard and tried to pound him into submission. Leonard tried to dance away and score points with jabs. When the 12-rounder ended, Leonard fell to his knees from exhaustion. Moments later, the referee raised his hand in victory.

Since then, Sugar Ray has won two more titles. And the saga continues.

On April 6, 1987, Leonard captured the middleweight championship—his third divisional title—in a close, 12-round decision against Marvelous Marvin Hagler.

Sugar Ray Leonard shortly before his fight with Marvin Hagler. His good looks and intelligence have doubtlessly contributed to his popular appeal.

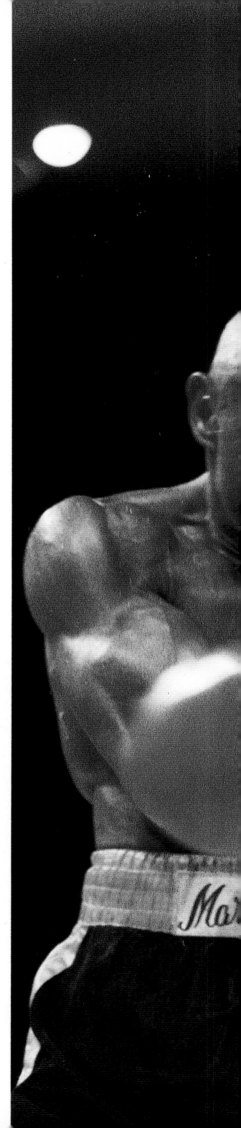

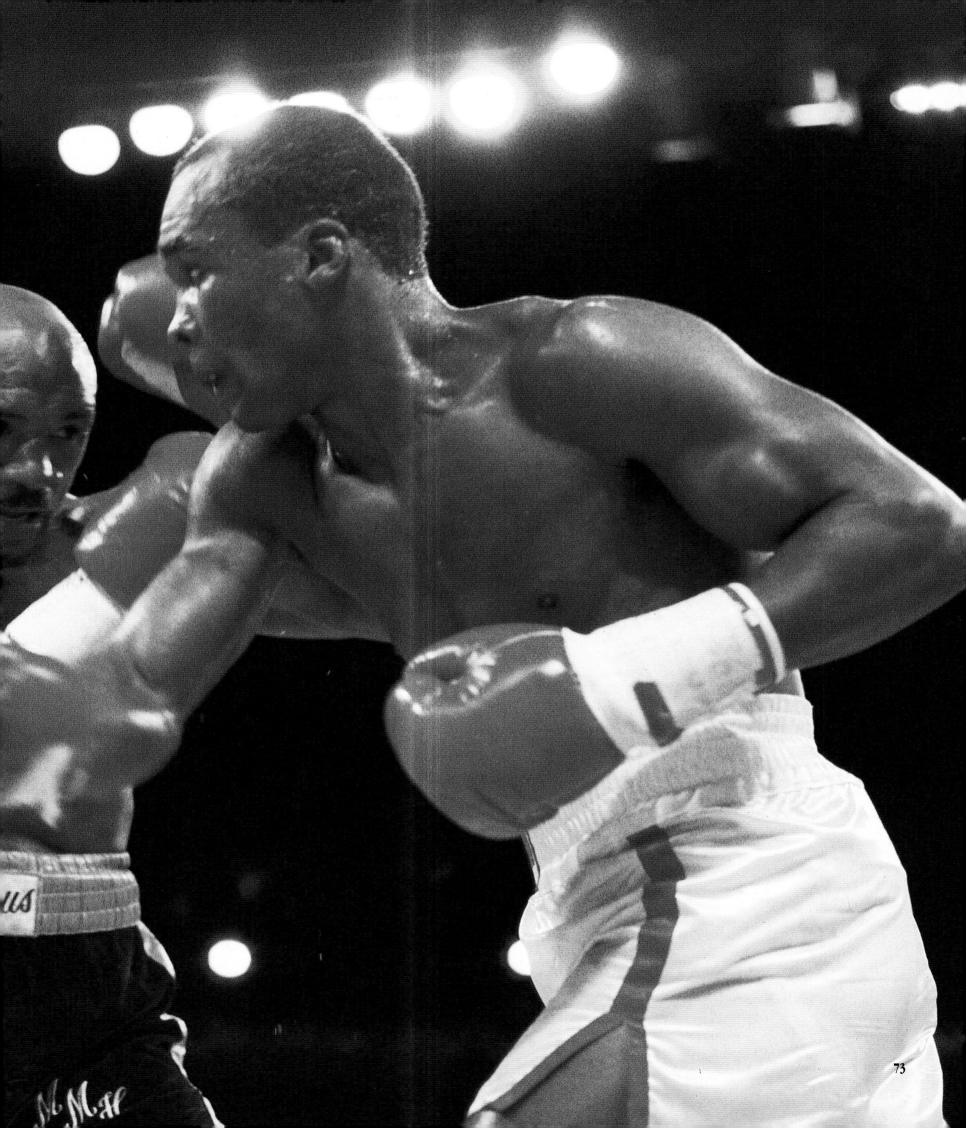

JOE LOUIS

ACTIVE YEARS 1934–1951

HIGHLIGHTS Amateur Athletic Union Light Heavyweight Champion (1934), undefeated World Heavyweight Champion (1937–1949), record of 63-3 (49 KOs)

Joe Louis Barrow, an Alabama sharecropper's son, grew up in Depression-era Detroit. Amateur boxing, with its pawnable medals, drew him into fighting at 16 and, by the time he was 20, he was the National AAU light heavyweight champ.

Louis turned professional and his rise was sensational. Starting with Jack Krackon on July 4, 1934, the "Brown Bomber" won 27 straight fights, 23 by knockout. Then, in July 1936, he was stopped in the 12th round by the veteran fighter and symbol of Nazi Germany, Max Schmeling.

Soon Louis was back on track however. He defeated former champ Jack Sharkey a month after the Schmeling fight and, on June 22, 1937, he captured the heavyweight crown by knocking out Jim Braddock in the eighth round. He was the youngest champ in heavyweight history and the second black. On June 22, 1938, he again met Schmeling. As before, the fight was held at Yankee Stadium. But this time, Louis brutalized the former champ in the first round which ended in a Schmeling defeat.

During the longest reign in heavyweight history, Louis defended his title 25 times, winning all but three of these contests by knockout. The parade of challengers was derisively called the "Bum of the Month Club" until Billy Conn arrived at the head of the line in June 1941. Conn, a clever boxer, nearly upset the champ. In fact, he was ahead on points when he tried for a knockout in the 13th round. Instead, Louis scored the KO.

Six months later came the bombing of Pearl Harbor and early 1942 saw Louis

In 1946, Joe Louis returned from a stint in the U.S. Army, to resume his position as heavyweight champion of the world.

enter the U.S. army. During the war, he fought two matches, giving his purses to navy and army charities. He also held exhibitions around the world and served as a boxing instructor.

Back in civilian life, he fought an anticipated rematch with Conn, whom he defeated easily, and won a disputed split decision against Joe Walcott late in 1947. Two years later, after a rematch in which he knocked out Jersey Joe, he retired as an undefeated champ. In 1950, however, tax indebtedness led Joe back to the ring where he lost a 15-round decision to the new champ, Ezzard Charles. A very old

Louis tried again, on October 26, 1951, this time against the relentless new boxing star, Rocky Marciano, and was knocked out in the eighth round.

Joe Louis's retirement years were eased by friends and with a job in Las Vegas where he died, at 67, in 1981.

(Right) On June 22, 1938, Louis avenged his 1936 loss to Max Schmeling by knocking out the former champ in the first round.

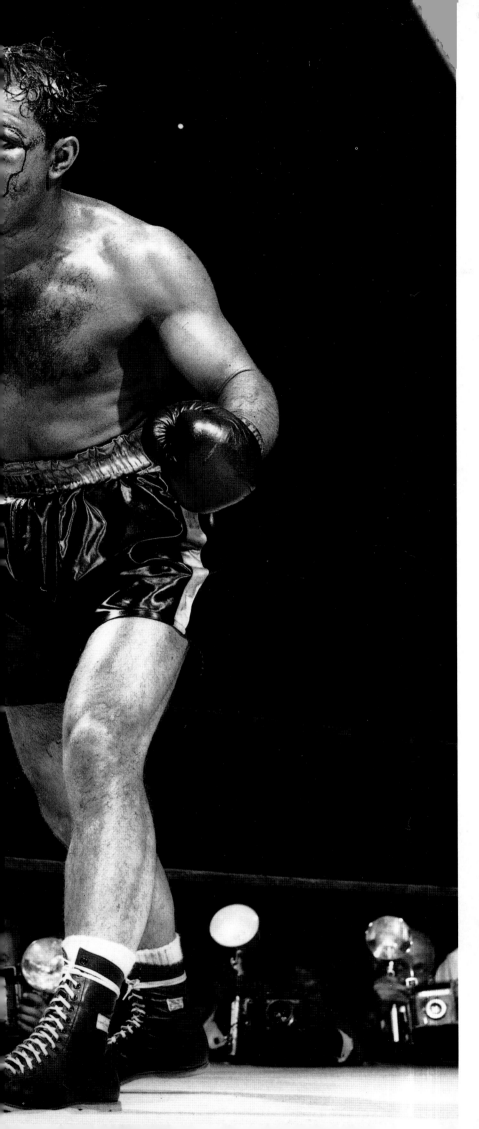

ROCKY MARCIANO

ACTIVE YEARS 1947–1955

HIGHLIGHTS World Heavyweight Champion (1952–1955), a record of 49—0 (43 KOs), judged "Best Heavyweight of All Time" (over Muhammad Ali) in computerized competition in 1969

At 5 feet 11 inches and 185 pounds, Rocco Francis Marchegiano was small for a heavyweight, but his punchng power was devastating. Initially the "Brockton Bull," a first-generation Italian from New England, had his eye on a baseball career but, when the Chicago Cubs rejected him in 1946, he turned to the professional ring, having fought amateur bouts in the U.S. army during World War II.

The unskilled Marciano caught the eye of Al Weill, a New York promoter and manager and, under the tutelage of trainer Charlie Goldman, learned to box. No one had to teach him how to hit. After a heavy schedule of small-time, east coast fights, he gained the national spotlight by taking on the great former champ, Joe Louis.

Louis, badly in need of a purse to pay off his back taxes, was knocked out by Marciano in the eighth round. The Rock was sorry to send Louis into permanent exile, but he knew that a rising contender usually had to climb over a fallen

(Left) *With blood flowing from his left eye, Marciano continues to battle contender Ezzard Charles in the sixth round of their June 17, 1954, fight.*

ex-champ. He promised himself that would not become *his* fate.

Rocky fought on, eliminating the top contenders in a record 42 victories in a row—all but five by knockout. Finally, on September 23, 1952, he met the champ, Jersey Joe Walcott. For 12 rounds Walcott gave the contender a vicious body beating, becoming the first to knock the Rock down, but, in round 13 Marciano landed a blockbuster and Walcott crumbled. *(See photo, pages 62–63.)* At age 29, Rocky Marciano became the heavyweight champ.

Walcott fought Marciano again the following May but failed to last the first round. Rocky next polished off Roland LaStarza, he twice beat former champ Ezzard Charles, and he knocked out British champ Don Cockell. On June 22, 1955, he took on the aging king of the light heavyweights, Archie Moore, in a contest that was a brawl from the opening gong. For only the second time in his career, Rocky was knocked down, but he got up to deck Moore four times, finally knocking him out in the ninth round.

Seven months later Rocky Marciano retired. During his entire career, through 49 professional fights, he never lost, an amazing accomplishment. Once he hung up his gloves, he kept the promise he had made to his family and stayed out of the ring. Then, on a summer's evening in 1969, he stepped into a private plane to fly home and was killed when it crashed.

A triumphant Rocky Marciano raises his hands in victory after his third title defense, a 15-round bout against Ezzard Charles.

SUGAR RAY ROBINSON

ACTIVE YEARS 1940-1965

HIGHLIGHTS New York Golden Gloves Champion (Featherweight, 1939; Lightweight, 1940), World Welterweight Champion (1946-1951), five-time World Middleweight Champion (2/14/51-7/10/51, 9/12/51-12/18/52, 12/9/55-1/2/57, 5/1/57-9/23/57, 3/25/58-1/23/60), a record of 175-29 (109 KOs)

H e was born Walker Smith in 1920 but as Ray Robinson—the name he appropriated in his late teens from another boxer's ID card—he became what many consider the greatest boxer, pound-for-pound, in the history of the ring. In a career that lasted 25 years, he had 202 fights, won 75 and failed to go the distance only once, due to heat prostration.

Following 85 wins as an amateur, including the 1939 Golden Golves feather-weight title, he turned professional in 1940. His winning streak continued through 40 more fights, 29 by knockouts. Then, in 1943, he lost to the "Raging Bull," Jake LaMotta. Three weeks later he defeated LaMotta with whom he fought six bruising battles during his career.

At the end of 1946, Sugar Ray won the welterweight championship—the first of his six world boxing titles—in a decision against Tommy Bell, but tragedy marred his first defense when Jimmy Doyle died after a knockout. In 1951, after successfully defending his crown against all comers, he gave up the championship to take the middleweight title from Jake LaMotta.

The pugilistic trail of Sugar Ray Robinson requires a boxing atlas to trace. From 1951 to 1960, he lost and regained the middleweight championship five different times. In 1952 he almost added the light heavyweight crown worn by Joey Maxim. Ray led into the final rounds of the outdoor fight in New York, where the sultry evening's temperature was over 100 degrees. Finally, the heat did him in and he failed to answer the bell for the 14th round.

Meanwhile, the handsome fighter was enjoying his four million dollars in purses. He drove a fuchsia Cadillac through Harlem, where he owned several businesses. When he visited Europe, an entourage went with him. And, as a tap-dancing protégé of Bill "Bojangles" Robinson, he headed a nightclub act between fights.

Then age caught up with the flashy 40-year-old champ and he lost his title, on January 22, 1960, to an unheralded Boston fighter, Paul Pender. Sugar Ray fought on,

meeting lesser known opponents in out-of-the-way places. Finally, in 1965, with his wife Millie, he settled down in Los Angeles, using his sports and show business contacts to start the Sugar Ray Robinson Youth Foundation. He died in April 1989 at age 67.

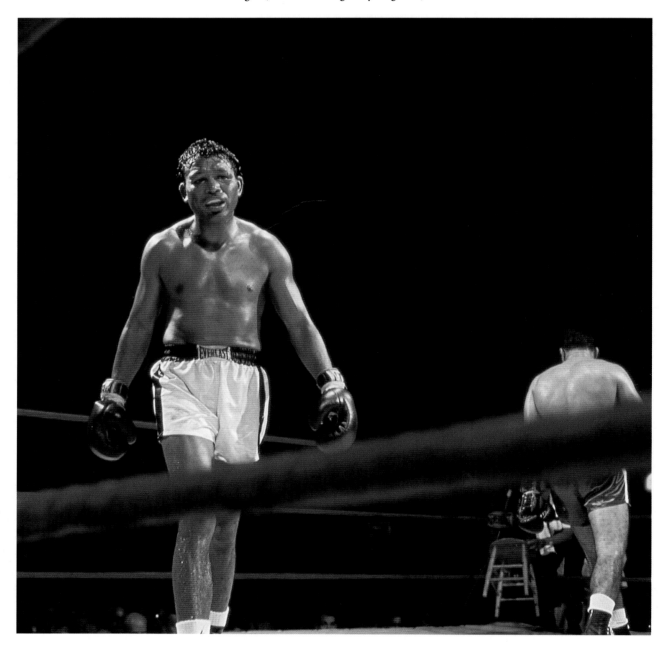

During his 25-year career, Sugar Ray Robinson won 175 fights and failed to go the distance only once, due to heat prostration. Pound-for-pound, he may have been the best boxer of all time.

GENE TUNNEY

ACTIVE YEARS 1919–1927

HIGHLIGHTS Light Heavyweight Champion—American Expeditionary Forces (France) (1918), American Light Heavyweight Champion (1922), regained (1923), World Heavyweight Champion (1926–1928), a record of 65–2–1 (43 KOs)

James Joseph Tunney, an altar boy from the parochial schools of New York's Greenwich Village, was the clean-cut antithesis of the fight game's brawlers. He had matinee-idol good looks and trained his lithe body into a tireless fighting machine. More a boxer than a power puncher, he lacked the popular appeal of a Jack Dempsey whose title he won and kept in two classic matches. But, unlike the "Manassa Mauler," who ducked military service during World War I, Tunney saw combat in France. He also became the American Expeditionary Force's light heavyweight champion.

When he returned home in 1919, the "Fighting Marine" turned pro. After 29 victories, he beat Battling Levinsky for the light heavyweight title on January 13, 1922. Later that year, however, he lost the championship to Harry Greb, a wily ring tactician with a two-handed, whirlwind style. Greb, who had given Tunney the worst beating he ever suffered, could have become Gene's nemesis, but the studious Tunney learned how to use Greb's style against him. When the two

met a few months later, he regained his title, defeated Greb in a third fight, and was ready to campaign as a heavyweight.

When Gene Tunney met Jack Dempsey in Philadelphia on September 23, 1926, the "Manassa Mauler" had been idle for three years. He was no longer the devastating fighting machine he had been, and Tunney, expected to lose by most observers, coolly boxed his way to an easy victory. Fight fans were stunned, and a rematch was demanded. It was held at Soldiers Field, in Chicago, on September 22, 1927. In what became known as the "long count fight," Dempsey, who was behind on points, dropped Tunney in the seventh round with a long left hook. Then, while a stunned Tunney sat beside the ropes, referee Dave Barry delayed counting until Dempsey went to a neutral corner as the rules required. An estimated 14 seconds later, a revived Tunney bounded to his feet and backpeddled out of danger. A lunging Dempsey chased Tunney the rest of the fight

but was cut to ribbons by sharp jabs and slashing crosses.

Tunney defended his title once more—against Tom Heeney, on July 26, 1928. Then a millionaire, he retired. Instead of boxing, he chose to pursue his cultural interests and a business career. He married an heiress, Polly Lander, of Greenwich, Connecticut, and later their son John was elected to the U.S. Senate from California. During World War II, the "Fighting Marine," now commissioned a captain in the U.S. navy, was in charge of physical training for the service.

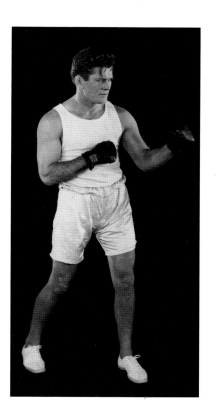

(Right) *Despite his handsome face and elegant style, Gene Tunney never reached rival Jack Dempsey's level of popularity. It was an era that revered power punchers more than boxers.*

The famous "long count" in the Dempsey-Tunney rematch, September 10, 1927. After waiting for Dempsey to reach a neutral corner, referee Dave Barry is seen reaching the count of nine as Tunney begins to rise.

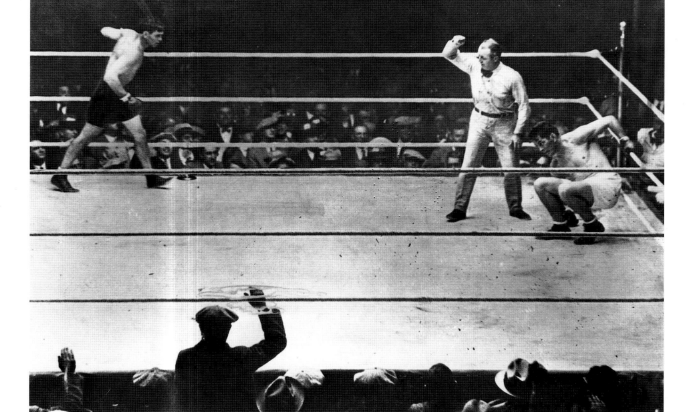

MIKE TYSON

ACTIVE YEARS 1985–

HIGHLIGHTS WBC heavyweight champion (1986–), WBA heavyweight champion (1987–), IBF heavyweight champion (1987–), 36–0 lifetime record (32 KOs)

E ven before he became the heavyweight champion, Mike Tyson had been a boxing historian. He studied the lives and watched the films of all the great fighters—Joe Louis, Rocky Marciano, Muhammad Ali. Tyson's name is destined to appear in the history books alongside the names of these legendary boxers.

Like many other fighters, Tyson was a child of poverty. He was born into a fatherless household in the Bedford-Stuyvesant section of Brooklyn in 1966, and he grew up as a tough kid on those mean streets. At age 13, he was sent to a reform school in upstate New York. There a former Golden Gloves champ, Bob Stewart, became his counselor and sparked his interest in boxing.

Stewart introduced Tyson to Cus D'Amato, the legendary boxing trainer, who eventually became Tyson's legal guardian and manager. D'Amato's goal was a spot for Mike on the 1984 Olympic team, but two losses in the qualifying rounds relegated him to an alternate's status.

In March 1985, Tyson turned pro and immediately began to build a name for himself by winning 11 of his first 15 fights by first-round knockouts. He had already developed his relentless pitbull style, punctuated by devastating uppercut punches. At 5 feet 11½ inches and 215 pounds he is smaller than many heavyweights, but no boxer today punches harder.

Tyson's first title victory came in November 1986 when he knocked out WBC heavyweight champion Trevor Berbick in the second round. Six months later, Tyson demolished the WBA title holder, Pinklon Thomas, in the sixth round. On August 1, 1987, he solidified his title by winning a 12-round decision over Tony Tucker, the IBF champion.

Since becoming the undisputed world heavyweight champ, Tyson has defended his titles four times. Most notably, he floored the ex-champ, Larry Holmes, three times in the fourth round of their bout on January 22, 1988, and laid out Michael Spinks in 91 seconds in their bout on June 27, 1988.

Despite his successes in the ring, Tyson's life has been unenviably tumultuous. A stormy marriage and divorce with actress Robin Givens, an automobile accident, and a series of battles with managers and handlers have kept Tyson's picture in the tabloids. But he has not lost his ring skills: on February 25, 1989, he demolished Frank Bruno, a talented British fighter, after an 8-month layoff. Mike Tyson is likely to be world heavyweight champion for a long time.

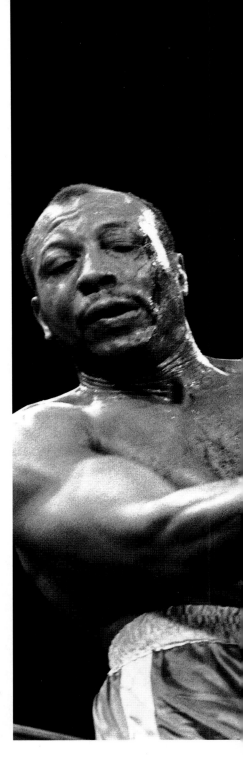

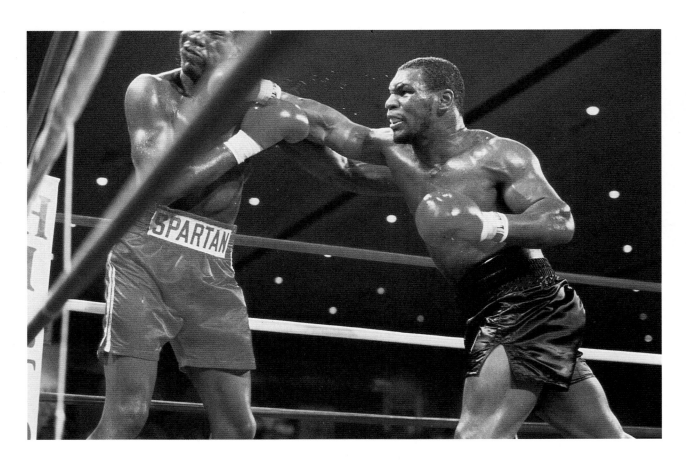

Following this bout with IBF champ Tony Tucker on August 1, 1987, Mike Tyson became the undisputed heavyweight champion of the world.

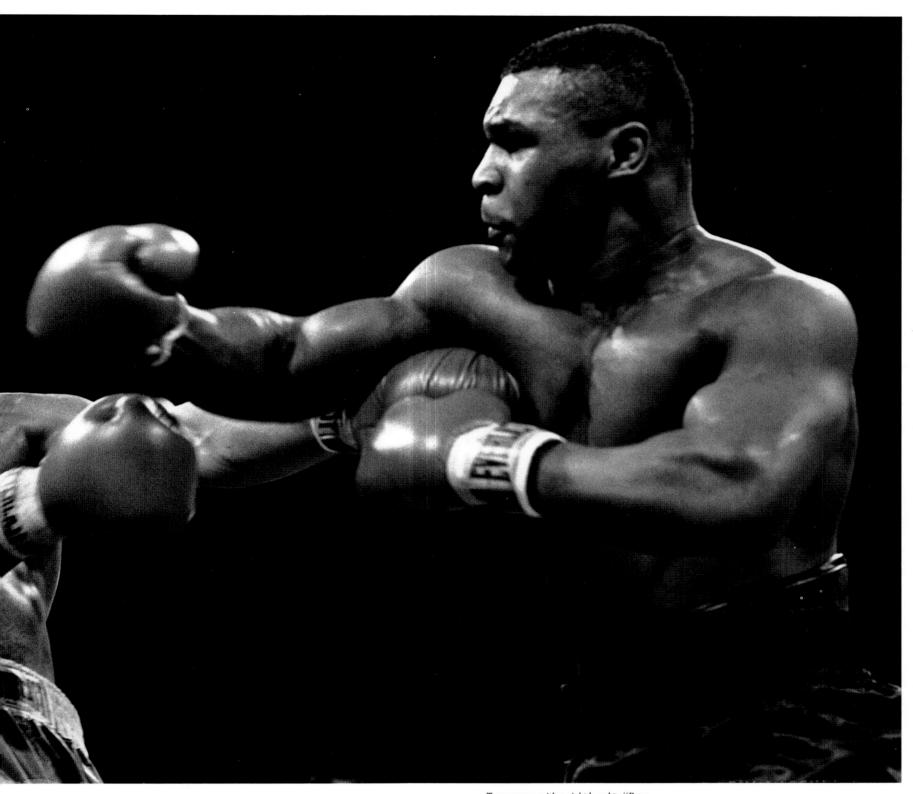

Tyson scores with a right hand to "Bone-crusher" Smith's cheek in their March 1987 battle in Las Vegas. Tyson won with a 15-round decision.

FOOTBALL

Sammy Baugh, seen here as a rookie in 1937, showed the run-oriented NFL the power of the pass and changed the game of pro football thereafter.

(Preceding pages) *O. J. Simpson takes on the Jets in the final game of 1973 and brings his total yardage for the year to 2,003, eclipsing the single-season rushing record held by Jim Brown. (See page 106.)*

SAMMY BAUGH

ACTIVE YEARS 1934–1952

HIGHLIGHTS All-American—Texas Christian University (1935, 1936), passing leader* (1937, 1940, 1943, 1945, 1949), punting leader* (1940–1943), lowest percentage of intercepted passes* (1940, 1942, 1944, 1945, 1947); *Professional Football Hall of Fame* (1963—Charter Member)

S linging Sammy Baugh taught himself to throw passes by aiming them through a swinging tire suspended from a tree outside his parents' home in Sweetwater, Texas. Born in 1914, he grew into a lanky 6-foot 3-inch collegian who set records at Texas Christian University in the pass-minded Southwest Conference. In 1937, the Washington Redskins, who had just moved from Boston, drafted the two-time All-American in the hope of impressing their new fans. He electrified them!

In the 1930s, professional football was primarily a running game but Sammy, who would pass anywhere at anytime, changed that. In his first NFL game, for example, he threw 16 times with 11 completions. In the NFL title

*National Football League

game that season, the rookie single-wing tailback, who was also the Redskins' kicker, stood in the end zone at snow-covered Wrigley Field urging the Bears—the team they called the "Monsters of the Midway"—to block his punt. Instead of kicking, he whipped out an unexpected pass that moved the ball almost to midfield and the Redskins went on to score, winning their first league championship.

Baugh was actually a superb kicker, who averaged 51.40 yards in 1940, the highest mark in NFL history. However, it was his slingshot throwing style that is remembered most; the lean and supple passer led the NFL six times in 16 campaigns.

Midway through his career, the Redskins converted to the T-formation and Slinging Sammy became even better with the new style of attack. The following year he completed a record 70.3 percent of his passes and led Washington to a divisional title. Two years later, in 1947, the fans held "Sammy Baugh Day." Rising to the occasion, Sammy passed for 355 yards, completing 25 passes—six of them for touchdowns!

Sammy Baugh played until age 38 when, after completing 11 straight passes against a frustrated Cardinal defense late in 1952, a big tackle, Don Joyce, slammed him to the ground, injuring Baugh's shoulder. The two players fought furiously and both were thrown off the field. It was Baugh's last game as a passer. A way had finally been found to stop him—get him kicked out for fighting!

GEORGE BLANDA

ACTIVE YEARS 1947–1958, 1960–1975

HIGHLIGHTS* Passing leader (1961), scoring leader (1967), MVP (1961, 1970), all-pro selection (1961), 236 touchdown passes (eighth on all-time list), 340 games played (first on all-time list), 2,002 points scored (first on all-time list); *Professional Football Hall of Fame* (1961)

*American Football League/Conference

A film of George Blanda's years in professional football would be titled *The Career That Would Not End.* The average life span of a pro football player is about five years; Blanda played for 25.

After an excellent career at the University of Kentucky, Blanda was signed by the Chicago Bears in 1949 to play quarterback and kick field goals. He played in Chicago for 10 years, a long but unspectacular career, and then retired. He had no idea that his best years were ahead of him.

When the new AFL began in 1960, Blanda went looking for a job and found one with the Oilers. He became the team's starting quarterback and kicker and led Houston to the AFL championship. In the 1960 title game, he threw three touchdown passes and kicked three field goals and three extra points in the 24–16 victory. The next season, he led the league in passing—throwing for 36 TDs—won the MVP, and again almost single-handedly won the AFL title game. In the 10–7 victory, he threw for the Oilers' only touchdown and kicked the extra point and game-winning field goal.

In 1966, the Oilers, sensing that Blanda's career was almost over, shipped the 39-year-old to Oakland. He played 10 more seasons!

In California, Blanda enjoyed the best of his 25 seasons. Midway through the 1970 season, he helped the Raiders tie the Chiefs by booting a last-second field goal, a big thrill for a 43-year-old man. The next week, he entered the game as quarterback in the fourth quarter, and with his team down 20-13, threw the game-tying touchdown pass, then kicked a game-winning 52-yard field goal with seconds remaining. The next Sunday, he came off the bench to drive Oakland to the winning touchdown in a 24-19 win over Denver. A week later, his last-second field goal beat San Diego, 20–17. Six times he drove his club from behind in the fourth quarter. In a losing cause in the AFC title game, he came off the bench for the injured Daryle Lamonica and threw for 271 yards and two touchdowns. For his efforts in 1970, he received the AFC MVP Award—at age 43.

Blanda played with the Raiders until 1975. He tried to make the club in 1976, but he was cut. So George Blanda, age 48, retired for good.

Though George Blanda played quarterback during most of his long football career, he may be remembered best for the 1,948 points that he scored as a kicker.

TERRY BRADSHAW

ACTIVE YEARS 1967–1983

HIGHLIGHTS led Pittsburgh Steelers to four Super Bowl Championships (1975, 1976, 1979, 1980), holds Super Bowl records for passing (932) and touchdown passes (9); *Professional Football Hall of Fame* (1989—first eligible year)

For a first-round draft choice, taken off the campus of Louisiana Tech by the Pittsburgh Steelers in 1970, Terry Bradshaw waited a long time for recognition. At first, his receivers got more credit for his completions than he did. Even when he led the Steelers to a Super Bowl victory in 1975, the spotlight focused more on owner Art Rooney, a beloved man who

had waited 42 years for a championship, than it did on the Shreveport-born quarterback.

The next year, when the Steelers won again, everyone thrilled to Lynn Swan's four spectacular catches. Even Terry's 64-yard touchdown pass, an impressive strong-armed throw, was lost amid the praise for Swan's dexterous reception.

Bradshaw continued to lead the Steelers through the 1970s. The star-studded team had an abundance of players to claim the spotlight. The balding, often bruised and battered warrior, Bradshaw, played more with a determination to win than in the flashy style of other NFL passers. In fact, he was perfectly willing to carry the ball and ran in 32 hard-earned touchdowns during his 14 NFL seasons.

When Terry Bradshaw got the Steelers into the Super Bowl again in 1979, his full value was finally recognized. Now it was his pinpoint accurate throwing the experts praised, not the 73 yards gained by the receiver after catching the ball. Certainly his performance in Super Bowl XIII was impressive. He gained 318 yards against a tough Dallas defense and was named the game's most valuable player.

The next year, against Los Angeles, Bradshaw was again the MVP, taking the Steelers to an unprecedented fourth Super Bowl championship and improving his all-time Super Bowl records to 932 passing yards and nine touchdown passes. After that zenith, injuries began

to slow Terry Bradshaw down and he retired following the 1983 season. Although his stardom came late, it did come, and he was ushered into the Pro Football Hall of Fame as soon as he became eligible in 1989.

(Below) *In Super Bowl XIII against Dallas, Terry Bradshaw, the game's MVP, completed 17 of 30 passes for 318 yards and four touchdowns.*

(Opposite) *Lacking the flash of other NFL quarterbacks, the strong-armed Bradshaw dug in year after year until his superb skills were finally given their due.*

JIMMY BROWN

ACTIVE YEARS 1954–1965

HIGHLIGHTS All-American—Syracuse (1956), Rookie of the Year* (1957), MVP* (1958, 1963, 1965), rushing leader* (1957-1961, 1963–1965), 12,312 career rushing yards (second on all-tme list), all-pro selection (1957–1961, 1963–1965); *Professional Football Hall of Fame* (1971)

J immy Brown is sometimes called the best lacrosse player that this country has ever seen—and records at Syracuse University seem to verify that statement. Most sports fans, however, know him as the Cleveland Browns' battering-ram fullback.

Brown was born in Georgia in 1936 and raised in Manhasset, Long Island, where his mother worked as a domestic. Brown earned 13 varsity letters and received scholarship offers from dozens of colleges. He chose to attend Syracuse, without a scholarship, and played football, basketball, lacrosse, and track. But football was his sport; he gained 986 yards his senior year and was named All-American.

Cleveland drafted Brown and immediately put him to work as their starting fullback. And work he did—battering NFL defenses for a league-leading 942 yards his rookie year. He followed in 1958 with 1,527 yards, exceeding the NFL record by more than 400 yards. When Brown entered the NFL, 1000-yard seasons were rare. Brown had one almost every year.

Brown's success was due to his great size and track-star speed. At 6 feet 1 inch and 232 pounds, he could rip through the line and run over linebackers. When he broke into the open field, he used his sprinter's speed to outrace defensive backs. And for a man who carried the ball so frequently, Brown also had great endurance. After a run, he rose from the turf slowly and limped back to the huddle, but in nine seasons he never missed a game.

Brown's best season came in 1963 when he rushed for 1,863 yards, a record that lasted until 1973 when O.J.

*National Football League

Jimmy Brown breaks through the line in the mud of San Francisco's Kezar Stadium as he takes on the 49ers in December 1962.

In 1965, at the top of his form, Brown called it quits, leaving others to ponder what he might have accomplished had he stayed in the game longer.

(Opposite) *As the Giants demonstrate, it usually took two or more defenders to bring down the powerful 232-pound running back.*

Simpson ran for 2,003. But Brown's most satisfying season was 1964, when his team won the NFL championship. In the title game against the Baltimore Colts, a 27–0 victory for Cleveland, Brown rushed for 114 yards.

At the end of the 1965 season, Brown, only 30 years old, retired to pursue a movie career. Two great backs of the 1970s, Simpson and Franco Harris (both wore Brown's number 32), threatened his career rushing record of 12,312 yards, and the greatest runner of the 1980s, Walter Payton, passed him. But anyone who saw Brown run with a football knows that no one did it with such flair.

DICK BUTKUS

ACTIVE YEARS 1962–1971

HIGHLIGHTS All-American—University of Illinois (1963, 1964), College Lineman of the Year (1964), all-pro selection (1965, 1968–1971), George Halas Trophy (1969, 1970); *Professional Football Hall of Fame* (1979)

Since the 1930s, the Chicago Bears have been known as the "Monsters of the Midway." Even during losing seasons, they played brutal, violent football. No one personified that style of play better than Dick Butkus, the Bears' rugged middle linebacker.

In 1965, George Halas, the Bears' owner and coach, drafted Butkus from the University of Illinois because the young linebacker had a reputation as a fierce, punishing tackler and an inspirational field leader—a man who could help turn the lackluster 5–9 Bears into a winner. Halas's decision was a good one. In 1965, the Bears finished 9–5. With Butkus leading the defense and another rookie, Gale Sayers, starring on offense, the Bears almost beat out the Packers and Colts for a division title.

Butkus became the leader of Halas's defense and the best middle linebacker in the NFL. Like all great middle linebackers—Sam Huff, Ray Nitschke, Joe Schmidt—Butkus was strong enough to push aside a 260-pound guard or tackle and flatten a 230-pound fullback. In fact, his jarring tackles earned him a reputation as the league's meanest player. But despite his 230 pounds, he was fast enough to run down an open-field ballcarrier or cover a speedy halfback on a pass pattern.

Batkus's NFL career was short; bad knees sent him to the sidelines in 1971 and eventually to the broadcasting booth. As a television analyst, he wears a jacket and tie and seems mild-mannered. But those who played in the NFL from 1965 through 1971 know better.

Dick Butkus puts a crushing tackle on Packer running back John Brockington in a November 1972 contest that the Bears lost 23–17.

ERIC DICKERSON

ACTIVE YEARS 1980–

HIGHLIGHTS* Rookie of the Year (1983), conference rushing leader (1983–1984, 1986–1988), all-pro selection (1983–1984, 1986, 1988), 9,915 lifetime rushing yards (sixth on all-time list), single-season rushing record holder (2,105 yards)

T he only active running back with a good chance to break Walter Payton's lifetime rushing record of 16,726 yards is Eric Dickerson of the Indianapolis Colts. After only six pro seasons, he is already more than halfway there!

He was born in the town of Sealy, Texas, in 1960 and starred on the local

*National Football League

high school team. Scouts from USC and Oklahoma wooed him, but the small-town kid wanted a college close to home. He chose Southern Methodist University in Dallas and had a fine collegiate career in a backfield that also featured Craig James, an All-America fullback.

At SMU, Dickerson shared running duties. But when the Los Angeles Rams drafted him in the first round in 1983, they installed a one-back offense with one objective in mind: give the ball as often as possible to the 6-foot 3-inch 218-pound rookie halfback. That season, he rushed for a league-leading 1,808 yards, with 18 touchdowns, and helped turn a so-so team into a playoff entry.

In 1984, his second pro season, Dickerson did even better—toping O.J. Simpson's single-season rushing record of 2,003 yards. That considerable accomplishment came in the 15th game of the season when Eric stampeded for 215 yards against the Oilers. He finished the season with 2,105 yards.

Although Dickerson quickly became pro football's leading rusher, the Rams traded him to the Colts in the middle of the 1987 season because of a contract dispute. As expected, he helped make a team of hapless losers into a playoff contender, and in both seasons with the Colts he led the American Conference in rushing.

The durable Dickerson should continue to pile up 1,000-yard seasons. He has the strength of a fullback and the speed and quickness of the league's fastest scatbacks. Although he might lack the sprinting ability of a young O.J., his acceleration through the line is without equal. If Eric Dickerson stays fit and maintains his form, sometime in the 1990s Payton's lifetime rushing record may well be broken.

On December 17, 1984, Eric Dickerson gained 215 yards against the Houston Oilers to break O.J. Simpson's single-season rushing record.

MIKE DITKA

ACTIVE YEARS 1959–1972

HIGHLIGHTS All-American—Pittsburgh (1960), NFL Rookie of the Year (1961), all-pro selection (1963, 1964); *Professional Football Hall of Fame* (1988)

A s a high school sophomore, Mike Ditka was cut from the Aliquippa, Pennsylvania, high school football team because he weighed only 135 pounds. Ten years later, when Ditka was the toughest tight end in the NFL, many opposing players wished that he had never returned to the gridiron.

Ditka grew big enough—6 feet 3 inches, 230 pounds—to become a two-way player at the University of Pittsburgh. He was a standout on defense, but George Halas, the Chicago Bears' owner and coach, drafted Ditka in 1961 to play tight end. Ditka responded with 56 receptions his rookie year and pleased Halas with his devastating blocking.

In 1963, the Bears won the NFL title and Ditka was a key contributor with 59 receptions. In 1964, he caught 75 passes, a record for a tight end.

Despite his ability, Ditka was a difficult player to coach. An argument with Halas in 1967 led to a trade to Philadelphia. Ditka also battled the Eagles' coach, Joe Kuharich, and was shipped to the Cowboys. In Dallas, coach Tom Landry put Ditka to good use, and the team won two NFL titles and a Super Bowl. When Ditka retired, Landry hired him as an assistant coach, and the Cowboys continued to win.

Halas brought Ditka back to Chicago as the Bears' head coach in 1982, where he inherited an undisciplined team and toughened it into a yearly play-off entry. His 1985 Bears won the Super Bowl.

Ditka suffered a heart attack during the 1988 season, but he missed only one game. Since that high school coach, no one has been able to keep Mike Ditka away from a football field.

Mike Ditka used his great hands and outstanding blocking ability to establish a new standard for tight ends in pro footfall.

RED GRANGE

ACTIVE YEARS 1923–1934

HIGHLIGHTS All-American—University of Illinois (1924, 1925), first $100,000 football contract, all-pro halfback (1930, 1933); *Professional Football Hall of Fame* (1963—Charter Member)

T he red-headed son of a small-town police chief was born in Wheaton, Illinois, on June 13, 1903. As a teenager, Harold Edward Grange delivered 200-pound blocks of ice from a wagon, building the strength that would eventually make him the University of Illinois' greatest halfback.

The "Galloping Ghost" had his best college game on the day that Illinois dedicated huge Memorial Stadium, October 18, 1929. On that warm afternoon, against archrival Michigan, Grange streaked 95 yards with the opening kickoff. Before the first quarter ended, he had scored three more times on runs of 67, 56, and 44 yards. Later he added a fifth touchdown and passed for another.

Grange, a 6-foot, 185-pound back, galloped through the Roaring '20s as college football's most glamorous contribution to the Golden Age of Sport. Saturday after Saturday he showed his extraordinary ball-carrying talent.

After his final Illini game, the man who had packed stadiums while a student turned professional, signing football's first $100,000 guaranteed contract with his home-state Chicago Bears. He joined the team for a Thanksgiving Day game watched by 36,000 at Wrigley Field. Three days later the Bears drew 28,000 in a snow storm. Then the Bears hit the road. In New York, playing the Giants, 65,000 people filled the Polo Grounds to see the famed "Ghost," the largest crowd to witness a pro football game to that time. In all, Red Grange played 17 games between December 2 and February 1, eight of them squeezed into 11 days!

Red Grange was one of pro football's first superstars, a key figure during the 1920s' Golden Age of Sports.

The next year Grange signed with a short-lived rival league but was injured and missed the 1928 season. However, in 1929 he was back with the Bears, for whom he played six years, four of them as an All-League halfback. In 1933 he starred in the first NFL championship game, which the Bears won, 23–21, over the New York Giants. Grange called it "the most exciting game I ever played." The winning player's share was $240, a pittance by today's standards, but in those Depression years, players without Grange's superstar salary were happy to get what they could.

Grange played football because he loved the game. He was smart enough to save most of the big money his celebrity brought and, upon retirement, he became a fine football broadcaster and businessman. He moved to Florida when he was 60. There, he enjoys a comfortable family life with fishing and golf his sports and football a happy memory.

At the University of Illinois, the "Galloping Ghost" thrilled cheering fans in game after game with his dazzling runs from scrimmage.

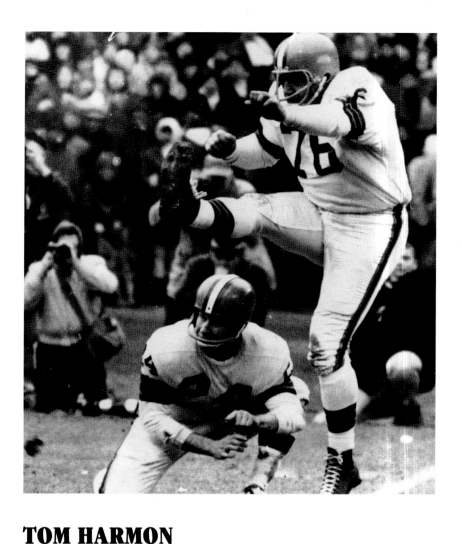

LOU GROZA

ACTIVE YEARS 1946–1967

HIGHLIGHTS leader in field goals* (1946, 1950, 1952–1954, 1957), leader in scoring* (1946, 1957), six times All-League offensive tackle, most seasons with one team, Cleveland Browns (21), second most points after touchdown (641); *Professional Football Hall of Fame* (1974)

O ne of the oversized Groza boys from Martins Ferry, West Virginia, Louis Ray developed into a great offensive tackle, but is best remembered as the "Toe," a tribute to his placekicking ability. In his 21-year career—spent entirely with the Cleveland Browns—he scored 1,608 points and led the league in field goals six times. Although he was acclaimed for

*National Football League/Conference

In 1964, Lou the "Toe" Groza kicked eight play-off field goals—a single-season record—as the Browns defeated the Colts in the championship game, 27–0.

his accuracy, the most dramatic moment of his career came as the result of a missed kick.

It was in the 1950 NFL championship game. Having missed an extra point in the first quarter due to a bad snap, Groza was called upon in the final seconds of the game to salvage the grudge match between the Cleveland Browns and the Los Angeles Rams. With only seconds left, and the Browns trailing by a point, they had the ball on the Rams' 16-yard line. This time the snap was true and Lou's kick accurate. The Browns won, 30–28, and went on to be an NFL powerhouse.

As the dynasty grew, new parts kept the Browns' machine running. Groza, now exclusively a kicker, remained until 1967, when he took off the squared-toed shoe for the last time. He left as the leading lifetime scorer. In the more than 20 years since, only George Blanda and Jan Stenerud have surpassed him.

TOM HARMON

ACTIVE YEARS 1938–1940, 1946–1947

HIGHLIGHTS All-American—Michigan University (1939, 1940), Heisman Trophy winner (1940), first draft choice—Chicago Bears (1941)

I t marks the passing of time and fame that a 70-year-old man, who was once the nation's most glamorous college football hero, is now best known as the father of actor Mark Harmon, the father-in-law of the late Ricky Nelson, and the grandfather of Tracy Nelson.

Tom Harmon was born in a small Indiana town, Rensselaer, but grew up in the iron mill city of Gary. The youngest of six children in a close-knit Irish family, he showed athletic ability early and chose Michigan's scholarship offer in 1938. The Big Ten was a powerful showcase for Harmon's talent. In 1940, he led the nation in scoring with 117 points, as he averaged two touchdowns per contest in an 8-game season. In addition to his rushing skill, he was a solid blocker and a

good open-field tackler. He was twice named All-American, and in 1940 won the Heisman Trophy by more than 800 points over his nearest competitor.

The clouds of World War II disrupted Harmon's prospects as the number one draft choice of the Chicago Bears. Instead, he became a pilot in the U.S. Army Air Force, where he survived two extraordinary crashes, one on a training flight over the South American jungle, and one in combat over China.

When the war ended, Harmon joined the Los Angeles Rams to try a delayed pro career, but his days of stardom were over. He showed a few flashes of his former brilliance, then retired to become a sportscaster, eventually as a member of the ABC sports staff, doing play-by-play accounts of nationally televised games.

In his three years as a tailback for the University of Michigan, Tom Harmon scored 33 touchdowns, was twice named All-American, and was the Heisman Trophy winner in 1940.

JERRY KRAMER

ACTIVE YEARS 1956–1968

HIGHLIGHTS all-pro selection (1960, 1962, 1963, 1966, 1967), member of five NFL championship teams (1961, 1962, 1965, 1966, 1967)

In Super Bowl II, Kramer escorts running back Donny Anderson upfield against the Oakland Raiders.

Most NFL offensive linemen labor in anonymity while the glory goes to the men who score touchdowns. Jerry Kramer, the hard-blocking 250-pound guard on the great Green Bay Packer teams of the 1960s, made so many key blocks that he became impossible to ignore.

When the 21-year-old Kramer came to Green Bay, via the University of Idaho in 1958, the Packers were a sorry bunch, a team headed for its second straight last-place finish. In 1959, however, coach Vince Lombardi came to Green Bay to build a winner.

Kramer was Lombardi's kind of player: talented, disciplined, hard-working, able to play with injury. Under Lombardi, the Packers became the NFL's best team, and Kramer became an all-pro guard.

Lombardi's coaching philosophy was simple: practice a few plays until they are executed perfectly every time. His favorite was the Green Bay power sweep, an end run by Jimmy Taylor or Paul Hornung with two pulling guards leading the way. No guard led the sweep better than Kramer. He was quick enough to pull to the outside before Hornung or Taylor and strong enough to clear away a big linebacker coming up to stop the play. With Kramer blocking, Taylor and Hornung enjoyed big seasons.

But Kramer got his share of recognition. Smart fans knew that his block on a power sweep sprung Hornung for a 13-yard touchdown and clinched the Packers' championship in 1965. Two years later, in the frigid title game

Jerry Kramer transcended the anonymity of most defensive linemen to gain deserved recognition, in part for his superb playing skills and in part for his best-selling book Instant Replay.

against Dallas, Kramer became famous with a block on Jethro Pugh that punctured a huge hole in the Cowboy line and allowed quarterback Bart Starr to sneak into the end zone for the game-winning touchdown with 13 seconds left on the clock. That key block was replayed again and again on T.V. Kramer later wrote in *Instant Replay,* his best-selling book on the 1967 season, "Millions of people who couldn't name a single offensive lineman if their lives depended on it heard my name repeated and repeated."

When Kramer retired after the 1968 season, he had five NFL championship rings.

JOE MONTANA

In Super Bowl XIX, Montana earned MVP honors as he racked up 331 yards passing and three TDs.

ACTIVE YEARS 1975–

HIGHLIGHTS* NFC passing leader (1984, 1985, 1987), all-pro selection (1981, 1985), Super Bowl MVP (1982, 1985)

The Johnny Unitas of today's quarterbacks is Joe Montana of the San Francisco 49ers. Like Unitas, "Golden Joe" has built a reputation as a big-play passer who saves his best performances for the biggest games.

He was born in the Pennsylvania hill country in 1956, and his boyhood idol was another Pennsylvanian, Joe Namath. Montana accepted a scholarship to Notre Dame, but he spent much of his collegiate career on the bench. Coach Dan Devine, however, often sent Montana into the fray with the team trailing late in the game, and Joe became known as the "Comeback Kid" for his ability to turn a sure defeat into a Notre Dame victory. His most famous performance came in the 1979 Cotton Bowl against Houston, when he brought the Fighting Irish from a 34–12 deficit late in the third quarter to a stunning 35–34 victory.

Pro scouts considered Montana too inconsistent for the NFL, but the 49ers drafted him in the third round in 1979. The next season he became a starter and

*National Football League

began to repeat his old Notre Dame tricks—bringing his team back from certain defeat with a series of fourth-quarter passes.

In 1981, Montana led the Niners to a conference championship, and in the NFC title game against Dallas, he solidified his reputation when he directed a game-winning 89-yard touchdown drive with only scant minutes to play. The winning touchdown, a pass to Dwight Clark with 51 seconds left, became known to Niner fans as "The Catch." Two weeks later, the 49ers won the Super Bowl, and Montana was named MVP.

Three years later, in 1985, Montana won his second Super Bowl MVP award when he gunned down the Dolphins, 38–16. His Dolphin counterpart, Dan Marino, was touted as the league's best quarterback, but Montana completed 24 of 35 passes for 331 yards and three TDs in the big game.

His 49ers were back in the Super Bowl in 1989, and Montana pulled off perhaps his greatest comeback. With 3:10 left to play and his club trailing the Bengals, 16–13, Montana engineered a 92-yard drive that culminated in a game-winning touchdown pass to John Taylor. In that game, Montana completed 23 of 37 passes for 357 yards (a Super Bowl record) and two TDs. Were it not for the splendid performance of his favorite receiver, Jerry Rice, Joe would almost certainly have gained yet another Super Bowl MVP award.

A 10-year NFL vet, Montana has some great years behind him and looks forward to some great years ahead. The game's most accurate passer, with a completion rate over 60 percent, the "Comeback Kid" is still most dangerous when the game is on the line.

(Following page) In Super Bowl XIX, Montana earned MVP honors as he racked up 331 yards passing and three TDs.

BRONKO NAGURSKI

ACTIVE YEARS 1927–1937, 1943

HIGHLIGHTS All-American—University of Minnesota (1928, 1929), all-pro selection (1932–1934, 1936, 1937); *Professional Football Hall of Fame* (1963—Charter Member)

T he great sportswriter Grantland Rice said Nagurski was perhaps the greatest college player of all time. Certainly the man they called Bronko was among the toughest.

He was born Branislaw Nagurski in 1908, the brawny son of Ukranian immigrants who farmed the challenging soil of northern Minnesota. In college, at the University of Minnesota, he put his 6-foot 2-inch frame and 230 pounds of muscle to work as a powerhouse fullback. When the other team had the ball, he became an impregnable tackle. Twice he was named an All-American at both positions.

In 1930, Bears coach George Halas brought Nagurski to Chicago, where he and teammate Red Grange created a legendary NFL franchise. The Bronk played lineman on defense and continued to rampage as a ball carrier. He was a devastating blocker, too, clearing the path in 1934 that let Beattie Feathers become the first player in NFL history to gain 1,000 yards. The Bronk piled up impressive statistics as well; in an era of 10-game schedules he totaled 4,031 yards in nine seasons.

In addition to running, Nagurski could use the short pass to gain extra yardage, stopping on bull-like plunges, leaping up and lobbing the ball to an open man. Initially he had to do so at least five yards behind the line of scrimmage; then the league realized pro football would be more exciting without such a limit and eliminated the rule.

Honors as an All-League fullback came to Nagurski every year between 1932 to 1936, except one, when a knee injury slowed him in 1935. Ultimately that mishap led the Bronk to retire in 1937. But he didn't leave sports. He became a professional wrestler and won 300 matches.

In 1943, when World War II depleted the playing ranks, the Bears brought Nagurski back as a lineman. However, it wasn't until the last game of the season, a showdown for the Western Conference title, that he saw action as a ballcarrier. In the fourth quarter, with the Bears trailing the Chicago Cardinals, 21–14, he repeatedly rammed the ball down the field to first tie and then win the game.

In the ensuing play-off against Washington, Nagurski's ball carrying was again the deciding factor as the Bears romped to a 41–21 victory.

Bronko Nagurski, shown here in 1929, was a superb all-around player: a gifted runner, a devastating blocker, a good short passer, and a dangerous defensive lineman.

JOE NAMATH

ACTIVE YEARS 1963–1977

HIGHLIGHTS Rookie of the Year* (1965), all-pro selection* (1968, 1972), MVP* (1968), Super Bowl MVP (1969); *Professional Football Hall of Fame* (1985)

H ow did a kid from Beaver Falls, Pennsylvania, become "Broadway Joe," the biggest celebrity in professional football? He used his good looks, his big mouth, and his strong passing arm to make himself famous and change the course of football history.

*American Football League

(Opposite) *His bit of stubble, fashionably long hair, and devilish grin helped earn Namath the nickname "Broadway Joe."*

By the time that kid, Joe Willie Namath, left the University of Alabama in 1965, he was about to become rich and famous. After an outstanding college career, Namath received an unprecedented $425,000 offer from Sonny Werblin to quarterback his AFL New York Jets. At the time, the NFL and AFL were still competing for the best college players, and Werblin assumed that Namath would give his young league instant recognition. Namath signed and set out to make good on Werblin's investment.

New York was the right place for Namath. He liked the night life and night clubs—hence the nickname. He grew his hair long, spent his money freely, and cavorted with society types.

He also played stellar football. As a rookie, he threw for 18 touchdowns and 2,200 yards. Two years later, in 1967, he became the first pro quarterback to throw for over 4,000 yards in a season. And his on-the-field personality matched his off-the-field lifestyle for devil-may-care living. He passed dangerously—ignoring the open man in the flat and whipping the ball deep down the middle. Interceptions came frequently, but the yardage and touchdowns piled up.

In 1968, Namath led his Jets to a division title, then gunned down the Raiders in a wild AFL title game, which gave the Jets a date with the Baltimore Colts in Super Bowl III on January 12, 1969.

In the first two Super Bowls, the AFL teams had lost by lopsided scores, and the pundits thought this one would end the same way. But a few days before the game, Broadway Joe arrogantly predicted a Jet victory. "I guarantee it," he told reporters.

Namath made his boast stand. He completed 17 of 28 passes for 206 yards and steadily guided the Jets to a 16–7 win. The pro football world was shocked, and from then on, AFL teams were taken seriously.

Namath never matched his achievements of the 1968/69 season. A series of knee injuries and the demise of the Jets kept him out of future Super Bowls. Nonetheless, he still threw for 173 lifetime touchdowns and tallied 27,663 yards passing—spectacular numbers for a kid from Beaver Falls.

In Super Bowl III, Joe Namath makes good his pregame prediction by leading the underdog Jets to a stunning upset over the Baltimore Colts.

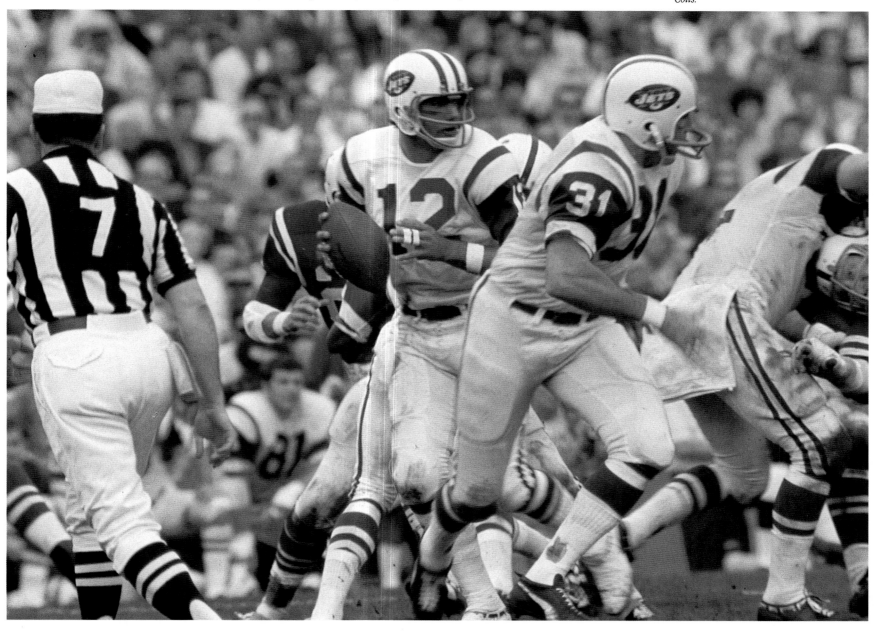

WALTER PAYTON

ACTIVE YEARS 1972–1987

HIGHLIGHTS* NFC rushing leader (1976–1980), MVP (1977, 1985), all-pro selection (1976–1980, 1984–1985), single-game rushing record (275 yards), 16,726 career rushing yards (first on all-time list)

T he man who broke Jimmy Brown's career rushing record was nicknamed "Sweetness." The name is one of football's great misnomers. Wherever he played, Walter Payton was one of the toughest men on the field. *(See photo, pages 2–3.)*

A Mississippi native, Payton was drafted by the Chicago Bears in 1975 after a fine college career at Jackson State University. The Bears were in a long slump, without a winning season since 1967. Payton spent much of his rookie year on the bench, and the Bears came up losers again, with a record of 4–10. Payton cracked the starting lineup in 1976 and made it evident to his teammates that losing was no longer acceptable. He rushed for a league-leading 1,390 yards, and the Bears finished 7–7.

The following year, Payton had his best season. He set a single-game record when he rushed for 275 yards against Minnesota and finished the season with 1,852 yards, an average of 5.5 yards per carry. He was a consensus all-pro and won the MVP award. Inspired by Payton, the Bears improved to 9–5.

In the ensuing years, the supporting cast sometimes changed, but Payton was always outstanding. He led his conference in rushing for five straight seasons, often operating behind a shaky offensive line or with quarterbacks who could not throw, thus allowing defenses to key on him. He was small—5 feet 10½ inches and 205 pounds—but he ran with great power, enabling him to stiff-arm and run over tacklers whom the blockers missed. Once in the open field, he could cut quickly. O.J. Simpson called him an "insane runner" who cut with-

*National Football League

out "rhyme or reason, but it all works out. It's an instinct."

In 1984, after eight 1,000-yard seasons, Payton broke Jimmy Brown's lifetime rushing record of 12,312 yards. But the highlight of his career came a year later when the Bears, after years of steady improvement, won the Super Bowl. Finally, Payton played for a winner.

He retired after the 1987 season with 16,726 career rushing yards, 4,000 more than Brown. He was, however, more than a ballcarrier. He was a punishing blocker, a talented pass receiver, and an accurate passer on halfback option plays—one of the best all-around talents in pro football history.

(Above right) *In 1976 Walter Payton made the most of his first year as a starter by gaining 1,390 yards and leading the league in rushing.*

(Below right) *In a light-hearted moment, Sweetness displays his ball-handling skill. More impressive perhaps were his ball-handling statistics, especially his career rushing record of 16,726 yards.*

(Opposite) *During Payton's 12 years with the Bears, his distinctive high-kicking style created innumerable headaches for the defenders employed to stop him.*

GALE SAYERS

ACTIVE YEARS 1962–1972

HIGHLIGHTS All-American—Kansas University (1963, 1964), Rookie of the Year* (1965), scoring leader* (1965), rushing leader* (1966, 1969), all-pro selection (1965–1969); *Professional Football Hall of Fame* (1977)

N o NFL rookie ever had more of an impact than Gale Sayers. In 1965, the first-round draft choice of the Chicago Bears gained 867 yards rushing (5.2 yards per carry), caught 29 passes for another 507 yards, and scored a record 22 touchdowns. He also ran back kicks and punts. Six weeks into the season, George Halas, the Bears'

*National Football League

owner and coach, was comparing Sayers to his great runner of seasons past, Red Grange.

Consider, for example, the season's 13th game against the San Francisco 49ers in which Sayers scored six touchdowns in the mud at Wrigley Field. The first came on a first-quarter 80-yard swing pass from quarterback Rudy Bukich. The second and third—runs of 21 and 7 yards, respectively—came just before halftime. In the second half, he scored three times: on a run from midfield, a one-yard plunge, and a dazzling 85-yard punt return. In total, he carried the ball for 336 yards—113 rushing, 89 on receptions, and 134 on punt runbacks—to give the Bears a 61–20 victory.

After that game, fans began taking the comparison with Grange seriously. The 22-year-old Sayers was 6 feet tall and weighed 200 pounds, and, like Grange, was fast and shifty. In an open field, he seemed able to cut and sidestep without changing speeds, leaving defenders tackling his shadow.

In 1966, he performed even better. He led the league in rushing—his total was 2,440 yards, including receptions and returns, an NFL record. In 1967, he had another all-pro season.

In 1968, a knee injury in the ninth game ended a splendid season. He returned to win the rushing title in 1969, but suffered another knee injury a

year later. After unsuccessful comeback attempts in 1971 and 1972, Sayers realized his career was over and retired.

In 1977, at age 34, Sayers became the youngest man ever elected to the Hall of Fame. In eight NFL seasons—five healthy ones—he had provided more thrills than any back since Red Grange.

(Below) *In this 1973 divisional play-off, Gale Sayers characteristically finds an open hole and rushes for 20 yards.*

(Opposite) *Sayers was the youngest player ever elected to the Pro Football Hall of Fame. Many consider him the finest halfback of all time.*

O.J. SIMPSON

ACTIVE YEARS 1967–1979

HIGHLIGHTS All-American—USC (1967, 1968), Heisman Trophy winner (1968), rushing leader* (1972–1976), all-pro selection (1972–1976), MVP* (1973), 11,236 career rushing yards (sixth on all-time list*); *Professional Football Hall of Fame* (1985)

In December 1973, a confident O.J. Simpson poses for the camera as he approaches Jim Brown's single-season rushing record of 1,743 yards.

T he University of Southern California has produced fine students and great running backs: Frank Gifford, Mike Garrett, Anthony Davis, Marcus Allen, and Charles White. But the best, by far, was the "Juice"—Orenthal James Simpson.

Simpson, who grew up in San Francisco during the 1950s, was a troublemaker as a youth. Fortunately, he channeled his troublemaking toward the football field. After two years at City College of San Francisco, he transferred to USC and made trouble for Trojan opponents, rushing for 3,187 yards in two varsity seasons. After his senior year, NFL coaches were clamoring for his services. He ran the hundred in 9.3, but, at 6 feet 1 inch and 212 pounds, he was much bigger than most scatbacks.

The Buffalo Bills, pro football's worst team, won draft rights to O.J. in 1969. Playing without a line to open holes or a quarterback to keep defenses honest, Simpson struggled through three unspectacular seasons.

In 1972, a new coach, Lou Saban, came to Buffalo and built the offense around O.J. That year, Simpson led the NFL in rushing with 1,251 yards. A year later, he carved his name into the NFL record books.

Simpson began the 1973 season with a record-setting 250-yard game against New England. By the final game, he was just 60 yards short of Jimmy Brown's single-season record. Undaunted, O.J. ripped through the Jet defense at snow-covered Shea Stadium, gaining 200 yards on 34 carries to finish with 2,003 yards, a new record. *(See photo, pages 82–83.)*

The Bills never reached the Super Bowl, but their star halfback turned in several brilliant seasons and some unforgettable games. Early in 1975, the year he rushed for a record 23 touchdowns, Simpson gained 227 yards in a 30–21 upset against the Steelers, the league's best defense. On Thanksgiving Day in 1976, he set a single-game rushing record with 273 yards.

Slowed by injuries, O.J. retired in 1978 after a year with San Francisco. One of the top rushers of all time, he is second to none in natural talent.

*American Football League

BART STARR

ACTIVE YEARS 1954–1971

HIGHLIGHTS passing leader* (1962, 1964, 1966), MVP* (1966), all-pro selection (1966), Super Bowl MVP (1967, 1968); *Professional Football Hall of Fame* (1977)

S ome of Bart Starr's contemporaries—Johnny Unitas, John Brodie, Sonny Jurgensen— might have been better passers, but as a field general Starr was without peer. In his 16 seasons with the Green Bay Packers, he patiently guided the team to five NFL titles and two Super Bowl victories.

Starr walked a rough road to reach the top. Born in Birmingham in 1934, he dreamed of quarterbacking the University of Alabama to a National Championship. He did become the Crimson Tide's passer, but he spent his senior year on the bench. After graduating from Alabama in 1956, he was signed by Green Bay, but he spent two years as a second stringer, watching his team finish in last place.

In 1959, Vince Lombardi became the Packer coach, and Starr became his starting quarterback. Under their direction, the Packers became the best team of the new decade. They won a divisional title in 1960 and the league championship in 1961 and again in 1965.

The efficient Packer offense relied more on its hard-running backs, Jimmy Taylor and Paul Hornung, than on the passing of Starr, but Starr's contributions to the offense were always obvious. He could throw short passes with amazing accuracy to complement the ground game, or he could fire deep when circumstances demanded it.

In the 1966 title game against the Dallas Cowboys, for example, Starr lead the Packers to a 34–27 shootout victory

*National Football League

by throwing for 304 yards and four touchdowns. Two weeks later in Super Bowl I against the Kansas City Chiefs, Starr, the game's MVP, came out throwing with similar results: 16 of 23 passes, 250 yards, two TDs, and a 35–10 victory.

A year later, Starr was the hero in another Packer championship. In the NFL title game against Dallas, played in subzero weather, Starr, directed a masterfull 68-yard drive in the game's waning moments and then scored the

winning touchdown on a quarterback sneak with only seconds left on the clock. In Super Bowl II, he gunned down the Raiders and was again named the game's MVP.

Starr led the NFL in passing three times and retired with a sizzling 57.4 completion percentage and 152 touchdown passes. More important to Starr, however, were the five NFL titles that the Packers won while he directed the offense.

Although Green Bay was best known for its ground game, Bart Starr led the NFL in passing three times, with a completion record of 57.4 percent.

(Following pages) In Super Bowl II, Starr directed the powerful Packer offense to a decisive 33–14 victory over the Oakland Raiders and was named the game's MVP for the second year in a row.

ROGER STAUBACH

ACTIVE YEARS 1962–1964, 1969–1979

HIGHLIGHTS All-American—U.S. Naval Academy (1962, 1963), Heisman Trophy winner (1963), NFC passing leader (1971, 1977–1979), Super Bowl MVP (1972), all-pro selection (1971, 1976, 1977); *Professional Football Hall of Fame* (1985)

R oger Staubach did not play professional football until he was 27 years old. After a successful schoolboy career in Cincinnati where he was born in 1942, he entered the U.S.

(Opposite) The heart and soul of "America's team," clean-cut Roger Staubach was a Heisman Trophy winner, a graduate of the U.S. Naval Academy, and a superb quarterback.

Naval Academy, completed 63 percent of his passes, and became a two-time All-American. When he graduated from Annapolis, Midshipman Staubach owed the Pentagon six years of service, which delayed his entry into the NFL until 1969.

The Dallas Cowboys, who drafted Staubach, had to wait patiently while their future quarterback tossed about on naval warships. It was worth the wait. Staubach sat on the bench in 1969 and 1970, but the next year he became the Cowboys' starter and led the team to the championship. In the ensuing 24–3 Super Bowl victory over Miami, Staubach threw for two touchdowns and was named the game's MVP.

Under Staubach's direction, Dallas

became the NFC's best team. "America's team" they were called, because their multidimensinal offense won them fans everywhere.

The key to that offense was Staubach. He was a double threat who could move the team with his laser passes or scramble for key first downs when receivers were covered.

He was most dangerous when his team was down a few points and time was running out. Somehow he usually managed to get the ball into the end zone or close enough for a game-winning field goal. In the 1975 NFC title game against Minnesota, for example, Staubach hit his favorite last-minute receiver, Drew Pearson, with a 50-yard

bomb with less that a minute to play to give the Cowboys a 17–14 victory and a berth in Super Bowl X.

With Staubach at quarterback, the Cowboys won four NFC titles and two Super Bowls. In Super Bowl XII, the last time the Cowboys won the big game, Staubach was again the key performer: 17 of 25 passes, 183 yards, one touchdown.

Injuries forced Staubach into retirement after the 1979 season. He finished his career with a 57 percent completion rate and 153 touchdown passes.

In Super Bowl XII, Staubach earns MVP honors as he completes 17 of 25 passes, picking up 183 yards and scoring a touchdown.

FRAN TARKENTON

ACTIVE YEARS 1958–1978

HIGHLIGHTS passing leader* (1972, 1975), all-pro selection (1972, 1975, 1976), MVP* (1975), first on all-time list for pass attempts* (6,467), completions* (3,686), yards* (47,003), and touchdowns* (342); *Professional Football Hall of Fame* (1986)

B y the time Francis Asbury Tarkenton retired in 1979, he had broken all of Johnny Unitas's significant lifetime passing records—attempts, completions, yards, and touchdowns. Yet throughout his career, he had to contend with critics who said that he did not have a strong throwing arm.

*National Football Conference/League

During his early NFL years, Tarkenton was not known for his passing. He entered the league with the Minnesota Vikings in 1961 after an outstanding career at Georgia. The Vikings were an expansion team with a poor offensive line, and Tarkenton spent much of his time scrambling around in the backfield while he tried to find an open receiver downfield. Often enough, Tarkenton tucked the ball in and earned a first down himself. "Fran the Scram," they called him. In the days of dropback passers, Fran was an oddity.

But he could pass too. He led the league in passing twice and was always among the leaders. In a typical season, he was good for 2,800 yards and 20 touchdowns.

The Vikings traded Tarkenton to New York in 1967. The Giants had finished 1–12–1 the previous season, but Fran made the team respectable—earning them four straight second-place finishes, including a 9–5 record in 1970.

The Giants sent Fran back to Minnesota in 1972. By then, the Vikings had become contenders, and Tarkenton led them to four straight divisional titles and three NFC championships. During these seasons, Unitas's lifetime records began to fall. Tarkenton set the most prestigious—the record for lifetime touchdown passes—in 1975.

Despite these achievements, Tarkenton's career had three major disappoint-

ments: Super Bowls VIII, IX, and XI. Each time that he led the Vikings to the big game, the team was beaten by an outstanding AFC opponent. But the Vikings' coach during those years, Bud Grant, did not blame his star passer for losing. When Tarkenton retired in 1979, Grant called him "the greatest quarterback ever to play the game."

Fran Tarkenton puts on a typical display of skill and agility at the NFC title game in 1974 against the Los Angeles Rams.

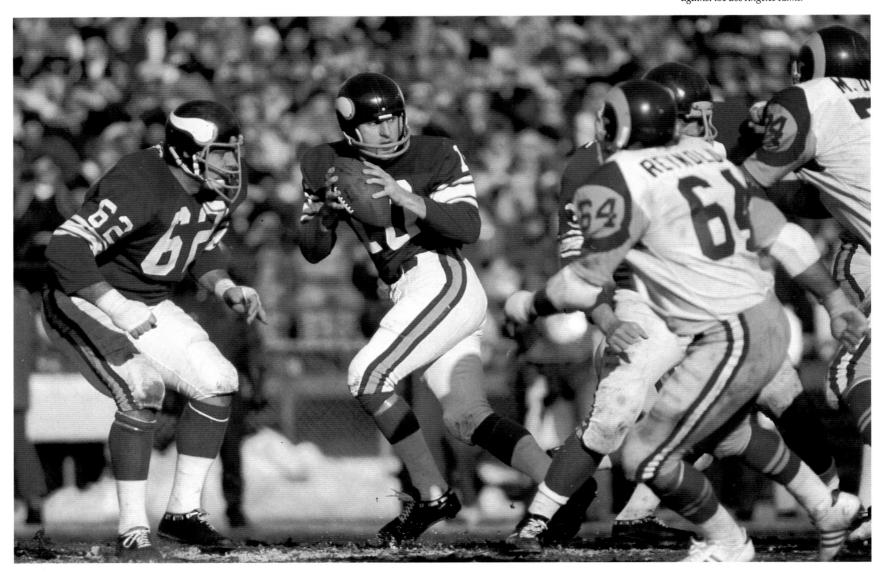

Y.A. TITTLE

ACTIVE YEARS 1948–1964

HIGHLIGHTS all-pro quarterbaek* (1961–1963), MVP* (1961, 1963), leader in touchdown passes* (1955, 1962, 1963), leader in passing* (1963); *Professional Football Hall of Fame* (1971)

Y ou could always spot Yelbert Abraham Tittle in pregame practice. He wore a red baseball cap while the others warmed up bareheaded. Y.A. was bald and feared that his lack of hair made him appear old. Actually, he had been known as the Bald Eagle since his days at LSU where the native of Louisiana first passed his way to national prominence.

Y.A. joined the NFL after two seasons in the old All-America Conference and became the San Francisco 49ers quarterback. When the team switched to a shot-

*National Football League

After 10 years with the 49ers, Y.A. Tittle finds new life in New York, taking the Giants to the top of the Eastern Division and earning MVP honors for himself.

gun offense, Y.A., at 34, was too old to run the ball as often as the new style required.

Fortunately for Tittle, the New York Giants needed a T-formation quarterback to replace the ancient Charley Conerly, and in 1961 Y.A. came east in search of the ultimate triumph—an NFL championship. His new team was loaded with great pass receivers, and Tittle used them well. In a game against the Washington Redskins, for example, he threw seven touchdown passes, tying the record. After the seventh TD, Tittle ran three more series of downs to end the game and remarkably did not pass once. It would have been showing off, he explained later.

That season, 1961, Y.A. Tittle led the Giants to the Eastern Division title while winning MVP honors. However, the team lost to Green Bay in the championship play-off, as it did the following year. In 1963, when Y.A. and Jim Brown shared the MVP trophy, it was the Chicago Bears who beat the Giants, 14–10. An intercepted pass, which the Bears ran back for a touchdown, stunned the Giants, and an embarrassed Tittle was denied a championship ring again.

He retired a year later, a passing master who was never quite successful at being in the right place at the right time—although his accurately thrown passes were.

Tittle looks like a contented man after his first season with the Giants in 1961.

JOHNNY UNITAS

ACTIVE YEARS 1953, 1954, 1956–1973

HIGHLIGHTS MVP* (1957, 1964, 1967), all-pro selection (1958, 1959, 1964, 1965, 1967), 290 touchdown passes (second on all-time list*), 40,239 yards passing (third on all-time list*), 2,830 completions (third on all-time list*); *Professional Football Hall of Fame* (1979)

I n his final years, Johnny Unitas set four new records every time he completed a touchdown pass—most passes attempted, most passes completed, most yards gained passing, most touchdown passes. Although his records have now been broken, Johnny U. is still known as ''Mr. Quarterback.''

Mr. Quarterback almost did not have an NFL career. The college powerhouses ignored the schoolboy record-setter from Pittsburgh because he weighed only 145 pounds. Unitas filled out, had a fine college career at Louisville, and was drafted by his hometown Steelers in 1955. But the Steelers did not see his

*National Football League

potential and cut him during training camp, so Unitas took a job as a riveter with a construction crew and quarterbacked the Bloomfield Rams, a semipro team, for $6 a game. The next February, Don Kellet, the Baltimore Colts' general manager, spent 80 cents on a phone call to invite Unitas to the team's training camp. Never did eight dimes bring a better return.

Unitas sat on the bench in 1956, but the next season he became a starter and won the league's MVP Award. In 1958, he led the Colts to a Western Division title—and a date with the New York Giants in the NFL championship game on December 28.

The 1958 title game is often called the greatest football game ever played, and Unitas is most responsible for that designation. Trailing 17–14 with less than two minutes remaining and the ball on the Colt 14-yard line, Unitas moved his team into position for the tying field goal with four pass completions, the last three to his favorite receiver, Ray Berry. Then in overtime, Unitas directed a brilliant 13-play, 80-yard drive that resulted in the winning touchdown. In

the pressure game, Unitas completed 26 of 40 passes for 349 yards. The following season he again gunned down the Giants in the NFL title game, 31–16.

Throughout the 1960s, Unitas was the NFL's best quarterback. His long bombs consistently dropped into the arms of streaking Colt receivers 50 or 60 yards downfield. His precision sideline passes with the clock winding down made him master of the two-minute drill. His inventive play-calling made him a field general with few peers. Since his retirement in 1973, pro football fans have seen some very good quarterbacks—but none better than Johnny Unitas, Mr. Quarterback.

(Below) *At age 36, quarterback Johnny Unitas directs the Baltimore Colts to a last-minute 16–13 victory over Dallas in Super Bowl V.*

(Right) *Unitas scrambles for 16 yards in the second quarter of the 1958 NFL championship contest, often called the greatest football game of all time.*

GOLF

BEN HOGAN

Ben Hogan proudly poses with his trophy from the 1948 PGA tournament.

ACTIVE YEARS 1931–1960

HIGHLIGHTS Masters champion (1951, 1953), U.S. Open champion (1948, 1950, 1951, 1953), British Open champion (1953), PGA champion (1946, 1948), PGA leading money winner (1941, 1942, 1946, 1948); *PGA World Golf Hall of Fame* (1974—Charter Member)

Bantam Ben Hogan actually weighed in as a middleweight at 160 pounds and hit golf balls like a pile-driving heavyweight. The wiry 5-foot 9-inch son of a village blacksmith had a golf swing that produced, in the opinion of Gene Sarazen—who saw them all in 50 years—the greatest game from tee to green of all time.

William Benjamin Hogan was 12 when his father died in 1924 and his mother moved the family from the tiny Texas town of Dublin to Fort Worth, where Ben helped support the family by becoming a caddy. In 1937, at age 19, he turned pro, but life wasn't easy for a young married golfer during the Depression and he didn't win a tournament for three years. From then on, however, he won with a regularity that others on the pro tour found monotonous and that the golfing public cheered. The perfection of his golf swing and his strategic skill were what drew the galleries, not his dour, unsmiling personality.

Hogan topped the PGA tour in earnings in 1941 and 1942, then became Lieutenant Hogan of the Army Air Corps. Four years later he came out of military service, won the PGA tournament, and resumed his place as the top money winner. Major titles continued to fall to his methodical attack until a near-fatal car smashup, early in 1949, left him with a battered body. Doctors said that he would never play golf again, his wired-together legs would never stalk a fairway. Yet, a year later, grim-faced with fatigue, he won the U.S. Open.

With iron resolve the indomitable Ben Hogan proved even better after his accident than he had been before, reaching, in 1953, the pinnacle of his career by winning the Masters (his second), the U.S. Open (his fourth), and the British Open in his first, and only, appearance. The Scots, a dour race themselves, nodded approval as Hogan broke the course record at Carnoustie, welcoming the businesslike invader and affectionately calling him the "Wee Ice Mon." Unfortunately, scheduling problems prevented him from playing in the fourth leg of the Grand Slam, the PGA. Still, no golfer has equaled his three-leg achievement.

Hogan's goal became a record-making fifth U.S. Open, but it eluded him. He came close in 1955 and 1956, as runner-up, then his putting game faltered. By 1960 he was freezing over the ball and retired from tournament play. Thereafter, he made infrequent appearances on the circuit, as in the 1967 Masters, when, at age 54, he shot a 66. He responded to the cheers by tipping the white cap he had worn as his trademark and shyly giving the gallery one of his rare smiles.

(Preceding pages) *In typically aggressive fashion, Arnold Palmer uses a sand wedge to get out of a bunker.* (See pages 126–127.)

BOBBY JONES

ACTIVE YEARS 1916–1930

HIGHLIGHTS U.S. Open champion (1923, 1926, 1929, 1930), British Open champion (1926, 1927, 1930), U.S. Amateur champion (1924, 1925, 1927, 1928, 1930), British Amateur champion (1930), only golfer to score Grand Slam (U.S. and British Opens and Amateur titles) (1930), established the Masters Tournament; *PGA World Golf Hall of Fame* (1974—Charter Member)

Robert Tyre Jones, Jr., learned golf the way little boys learn most things, by watching grown-ups. The precocious six-year-old would follow a Scot professional around the course; then Bobby, using a discarded wood-shafted cleek, would imitate what he had seen. In fact, he never had a golf lesson in his life. He didn't need one; he had a flawless swing and an instinctive understanding of the game. In 1916, as a self-taught 14-year-old, he played in the U.S. Amateur championship. Over the next seven years, Bobby often scored lowest in a tournament's opening round—against top professionals—but found that his immaturity and hot temper frequently prevented him from capitalizing on these early leads.

Finally, in 1923, at the age of 21, he won his first major tournament, the U.S. Open. The following year he won his first U.S. Amateur, and he kept on winning. In all, between 1923 and 1930, he won 12 of the major tournaments in the United States and Britian.

During these years Jones continued his studies so he could play in only a limited number of tournaments. But, in 1930, having graduated from Georgia Tech, earned a degree from Harvard and a law degree from Emory in Atlanta, he could concentrate full time on golf. That year he triumphantly won the Grand Slam, which included at the time the U.S. and British Opens and the U.S. and British Amateur championships.

Over the years, Jones had matured into a considerate, gentlemanly golfer, exceptionally modest yet consumed with a passionate need to play perfectly. Despite his triumphs of 1930, the pressure and tension of constant golf

were more than he wished to stand, and he retired to live quietly with his wife and three children.

In 1934 Bobby Jones gave a lasting legacy to the game—he helped design the Augusta National course and established the Masters Tournament. Until 1948, when he contracted a crippling spinal disease, he continued to play occasionally, sometimes flashing his old form, but mostly he just helped the Masters winner into the green coat given each year's champion.

Despite his infirmity, Jones remained a cheerful host and a gracious companion. He continued to attend the annual ceremonies of the tournament he founded until he was too wasted by illness to do so. He died in 1971 at 69, leaving not only the most impregnable record of all—his Grand Slam of Golf—but also the heritage of the Masters Tournament.

From a talented but hot-tempered teenager, Jones matured into a modest gentleman with a passionate desire to play golf perfectly.

Bobby Jones, captain of the 1922 U.S. Walker Cup team, leads his squad to victory in the first tournament of this American–British biennial.

BYRON NELSON

In 1943, when this photo was taken, Byron Nelson was at the top of his form.

ACTIVE YEARS 1930–1955

HIGHLIGHTS U.S. Open champion (1939), PGA champion (1940, 1945), Masters champion (1937, 1942), U.S. Athlete of the Year (1944, 1945); *PGA World Golf Hall of Fame* (1974—Charter Member)

John Byron Nelson, Jr., inevitably called Lord Byron, was born in Fort Worth, Texas, on February 4, 1912. He was only 18 when he won the Southwest Amateur championship. Over the next 25 years, he would win 61 more tournaments.

His peak performance years came in the 1940s. While most of the competitors saw military service, Nelson, a hemophiliac, was classified 4-F. Making the most of his opportunities, he won seven tournaments in 1944, averaging 69.67 strokes for 85 rounds and emerging as the PGA's leading money winner. In 1945, he won 19 tournaments, including 11 in succession. By the end of that two-year span, he had finished in the money in 113 consecutive tournaments; thus, many believe he was the greatest tournament player in the history of the sport.

Nelson's detractors maintain that his greatest number of victories came during the relatively competition-free years of World War II. No doubt he would still have had his share of triumphs against stronger rivals. And he would have been able to compete in—and perhaps win—tournaments that were suspended during the war, including the 1940–1945 British Open, the 1943–1945 U.S. Open, and the 1943–1945 Masters.

In 1948, Nelson retired from full-time golf. Like Bobby Jones, he found the weekly demands of the pro tour a burden. Had he played for modern prize money he could have coasted for many years, but the reality of mid-century golf was such that high annual earnings could only be found through the accumulation of many small purses.

After his semiretirement, he remained a distinguished presence along the tour. He played an occasional tournament—he won the French Open in 1955. But, for the most part, he has been content to coach and encourage young players, including five-time British Open champion Tom Watson.

JACK NICKLAUS

ACTIVE YEARS 1959–

HIGHLIGHTS U.S. Amateur champion (1959, 1961), NCAA champion (1961), Masters champion (1963, 1965, 1966, 1972, 1975, 1986), U.S. Open champion (1962, 1967, 1972, 1980), PGA champion (1962, 1971, 1973, 1975, 1980) British Open champion (1966, 1970, 1978), leading money winner eight times; *PGA World Golf Hall of Fame* (1974—Charter Member)

W hen Bobby Jones, the golf immortal, saw young Jack Nicklaus chewing up the Augusta National course one day, he aptly commented, "He is playing a game with which I am not familiar." Jones was right; nobody has ever played golf like Jack Nicklaus.

The son of a golfing druggist from Columbus, Ohio, Nicklaus played his first round of nine holes at age 10 and shot a 51. At 13, Jack surprised his dad one day with a 69. Still a teenager, he became Ohio's best player; and, at 19, he won the 1959 U.S. Amateur.

When Nicklaus began playing big-time golf, Arnold Palmer was ruling the fairways. But it soon became evident that the crown would pass to Jack. Still an amateur, he dueled Palmer and Ben Hogan in the 1960 U.S. Open, and only a magnificient charge by Arnie denied Jack the prize. Two years later at the Open, Nicklaus, now a professional, ended Palmer's reign by beating him in a play-off.

Nicklaus differed from Palmer in both style and temperament. While Arnie drove into the rough, then recovered by slamming a one-iron through a grove of trees, Jack was consistent; he played in the fairway and hit lovely iron shots to the green. While Arnie played in a rush, Jack studied each shot thoughtfully. Of course, Nicklaus was the bigger man— he weighed 225 when he turned pro but later trimmed down to 180—and he drove the ball much further.

From 1965 through 1980, Nicklaus was golf's best player, winning 17 major titles during that 15-year period, a record unmatched in golf history. But his sweetest victory came several years later.

Nicklaus began the 1986 season with poor performances in all the tournaments he entered; fans and players were whispering the word "retirement."

At the Masters, Nicklaus played well, but he trailed the leaders by four strokes after 54 holes and by five as he started the final nine. Suddenly he got hot— some splendid iron shots, some clutch putts, a string of birdies. The crowds screamed, the opposition folded, and Jack had another Masters—his sixth green jacket.

Nicklaus did not win a major title in 1987 or 1988, but no one is saying that he has won his last.

Jack Nicklaus contemplates a putt, with his son and caddy behind him during the 1986 Masters.

123

Nicklaus follows his approach to the green (opposite) *and celebrates the resultant putt* (left).

ARNOLD PALMER

ACTIVE YEARS 1954–

HIGHLIGHTS U.S. Amateur champion (1954), Masters champion (1958, 1960, 1962, 1964), U.S. Open champion (1960), British Open champion (1961, 1962), U.S. Ryder Cup team (1961, 1963, 1965, 1967, 1971, 1973), Associated Press Athlete of the Decade (1969); *PGA World Golf Hall of Fame* (1974—Charter Member)

A rnold Palmer emerged as golf's best player just as the game entered the television age. The result of this happy coincidence was that Palmer became a golf legend and the game soared in popularity.

The legend was born in Latrobe, Pennsylvania, in 1929. Palmer's father, an ex-steelworker who became greens-keeper and eventually golf pro at Latrobe Country Club, gave young Arnie a sawed-off club at age three, and became the youngster's first coach.

The first sign of excellence came in 1954 when Palmer won the U.S. Amateur title. The next year, he turned professional and won the Canadian Open. Within three years, he was a Masters champion and golf's leading money winner.

Palmer's reputation, however, was not established until 1960. In that year's Masters, he approached the 16th hole of the final round needing three birdies to win: he sank a 16-foot putt for his first on 16, holed a 30-footer for another on 17, then birdied the final hole to win the championship. Two months later at the U.S. Open, he trailed the leaders by seven strokes with 18 holes to play, but he played the front nine in 30 and took the title.

Those were Arnie's first famous charges—come-from-behind victories with only a handful of holes to play. Thereafter, golf fans knew Palmer, the slim man with huge hands and shoulders, as a swashbuckling daredevil who hitched up his pants, pulled out the one-iron, and went for the green. *(See photo,* *pages 116–117.)* Palmer's style of play attracted huge galleries—"Arnie's Army" they were called—and large television audiences which helped push golf's purses higher and higher.

Even when Palmer lost, he did it spectacularly. At Augusta in 1961, he double-bogeyed the final hole and handed the Masters title to Gary Player. In the 1966 U.S. Open, he blew a six-stroke lead to Billy Casper in the final six holes.

In the mid-1970s, Palmer was slowed by a hip injury that hindered his swing. Today, the first man to earn $1 million at the game of golf is semiretired, making TV commercials, living off his many successful business interests, and playing occasional PGA and seniors events. The galleries are still large, and he remains golf's greatest superstar.

Arnold Palmer tees off at the 1962 Masters
under the watchful gaze of his legion of fans.

Palmer studies his final putt at the 1958
Masters. He made the shot and won the tournament for his first Masters victory.

(Opposite) Palmer studies his final putt at the
1958 Masters. He made the shot and won the
tournament for his first Masters victory.

SAM SNEAD

ACTIVE YEARS 1935–

HIGHLIGHTS Masters champion (1949, 1952, 1954), British Open champion (1946), PGA champion (1942, 1949, 1951), Vardon Memorial Trophy winner (1938, 1949, 1950, 1955), U.S. Ryder Cup team (1937, 1938, 1947, 1949, 1951, 1953, 1955, 1959); *PGA World Golf Hall of Fame* (1974—Charter Member)

S am Snead made many converts to the game of golf. When nonplayers saw his smooth swing, they surmised that the game was easy. They found out differently, of course, but in the process they probably gained respect for Mr. Snead.

He was born on a Virginia farm in 1912, the same year that gave birth to Ben Hogan and Byron Nelson. A fine schoolboy athlete, Snead took up golf at age 15 when he began caddying and soon developed his classic swing. He began competing as an amateur in 1933. Two years later, in the middle of the Depression, he quit a restaurant job to become a full-time pro.

It took Snead only three years to reach the top. In 1937, he won his first important victories, the Bing Crosby and the Oakland Open. A year later, he earned a record $19,534 and was awarded the Vardon Trophy as the year's best golfer.

During the 1940s and 1950s, Snead was Mr. Golf. His record shows three Masters titles, a British Open win, and three PGA titles.

Although Snead is ranked among the top echelon of golfers, having won seven major tournaments in all, he never won the U.S. Open. Four times he placed second in that tournament. In the 1939 Open, he needed only a par-5 on the final hole to beat Nelson, but he hit a bunker, had trouble getting out, and three-putted for an 8. In 1947, he birdied the final hole to tie Lew Worsham, but on the 18th hole of the play-off, he blew a three-foot putt and lost by a stroke.

Lacking an Open title, Snead had to content himself with golf's greatest swing and a career unparalleled in longevity. In 1965, at age 52, he won the Greensboro Open and became the oldest player ever to win a PGA event. In the 1972 Masters, he stayed in contention through the final round; and in 1974—after years of victories on the seniors circuit—he played with the youngsters at the Los Angeles Open and placed second.

At age 77, Sam Snead is still playing golf. And the sweet swing still produces some good rounds.

Sixty-year-old Sam Snead displays jaunty confidence at the 1972 Masters. He remained in contention through the final round.

Snead demonstrates his unique putting style at the 1978 Masters.

TOM WATSON

ACTIVE YEARS 1969–

HIGHLIGHTS British Open champion (1975, 1977, 1980, 1982, 1983), Masters champion (1977, 1981), U.S. Open champion (1982), leading money winner (1977–1980), *PGA World Golf Hall of Fame* (1988)

His boyhood hero was Arnold Palmer, and early in his career he was tutored by Byron Nelson. Modest Tom Watson does not put himself in the same class as those two champions, but with 10 major titles already, and perhaps more to come, other people might well make such comparisons.

He was born in Kansas City, Missouri, in 1949 and was introduced to golf by his father, for whom he caddied. He won state titles as a teenager, played golf at Stanford, and finished fifth at the U.S. Amateur in 1969. In 1971, his senior year at Stanford, he turned pro.

By his own admission, Watson was not ready for professional golf when he joined the tour. His assessment was borne out the at the 1973 U.S. Open

when he scored a disastrous 79 on the tournament's final day after leading for three rounds. But under Byron Nelson's, tutelage his game began to improve. Two years later, he won his first major title, the British Open.

In 1975, Jack Nicklaus still ruled the fairways, but during the next seven years Watson engaged the "Golden Bear" in several memorable battles. At the 1977 Masters, for example, he beat Jack with a clutch birdie putt on the 17th hole of the final round. And, later that year, at the British Open, he matched Jack's 65 in the third round, then edged Jack 65–66 in the final round. On both days, the two played head-to-head, challenging each other with shots that dazzled the British Open fans. Four years later, at the 1981 Masters, Watson held off the charging Nicklaus by playing nine holes of almost perfect golf.

But Watson's most famous victory over Nicklaus came at the 1982 Open at Pebble Beach. Jack sat in the clubhouse with a final-round 69 and watched Watson's tee shot find the deep rough near the green on the par-3 17th hole. If Wat-

son had bogeyed the hole and parred the 18th, Jack would have had another U.S. Open title. But Watson used his sand wedge to chip the ball out of the high grass, then watched it roll into the cup for a birdie. He also birdied the 18th and won by three strokes.

Watson's last major title came in the 1983 British Open, his fifth victory in that classic event. Still, at age 40, he remains a contender in every tournament he enters. He may yet pull out a few more major titles from his bag of tricks.

(Below) *Tom Watson watches the roll of a putt at the British Open in 1977. He won the tournament over Jack Nicklaus in the final round.*

(Right) *Watson jumps for joy as he escapes the rough with a celebrated 17th hole chip shot that won the U.S. Open in 1982.*

BABE DIDRIKSON ZAHARIAS

ACTIVE YEARS 1930–1954

HIGHLIGHTS Dallas Women's Amateur Athletic Union National Basketball Championship (1930–1932), Women's American Track & Field Championship in six events (1932), Olympic gold medal winner—javelin throw, 80-meter high hurdles, high jump (disqual.) (1932), Woman Athlete of the Year (1932, 1945–1947, 1950), Associated Press Woman Athlete of the First Half of 20th Century (1950), U.S. Women's Amateur Golf champion (1946), British Women's Amateur Golf champion (1947), Women's World Golf champion (1949–1951), Women's Open champion (1948, 1950, 1954), leading female money winner (1948–1951); *PGA World Golf Hall of Fame* (1974—Charter Member)

A Texas tomboy, Mildred Didrikson ran roughshod over the ladies in the 1932 Olympics. The pickings were thin. Not only were there few events for women, each competitor could only enter three. The sports phenomenon that Dallas writers were already calling "Babe" for her exploits on the diamond, outran everyone in the 80-meter hurdles *(see photo, page 6)* outthrew them with the javelin, and outleaped them in the high jump. In the latter, however, officials ruled her head-first approach illegal and she was disqualified.

Babe was whippet-thin and fast, with rawhide strength and an arrogant way that hid her shyness. "Ah kin whump ya," she'd challenge her prom-bound competition. The press loved her, and publicity helped Babe earn her way through the mid-Depression years. While the sport purists snubbed her, she made vaudeville tours and played baseball with a barnstorming team against big leaguers.

Babe found her best sport was golf. Some money, as well as honors, could be won there, but for female golfers the 1930s were lean times. She toured the exhibition trail with champion golfer Gene Sarazen but was banned from the prestigious amateur tournaments by the U.S. Golf Association because of the money she earned playing basketball and baseball. Then, in 1944, her amateur status was reinstated, and she hit the circuit with a vengeance.

Soon she was cleaning up everything in sight. She won 17 straight tournaments and was unbeaten when, in 1947, she accepted a $300,000 movie contract and turned pro. Open titles and leading money status came her way as did a husband, wrestler-promoter George Zaharias. Then, in 1953, she developed cancer. She bravely came back from surgery to win the 1954 U.S. Open one last time, then died in 1956 at the age of 43. She was the greatest woman athlete of all time.

Didrikson poses with her javelin at the Olympic Stadium in Los Angeles, where she won the gold medal with a record-setting throw of 143 feet 4 inches.

A wan but smiling Didrikson poses for the camera shortly before her death from cancer in 1956. She was 43 years old.

(Opposite) *Babe Didrikson Zaharias is shown here in 1937, two years after she took up golf.*

ICE HOCKEY

In eight impressive seasons with the Bruins, Phil Esposito was voted MVP twice, but he is best remembered for the 76 goals he scored in 1970/71.

(Preceding pages) *Always ahead of the pack, Guy LaFleur dashes for a loose puck during a 1979 game against the Islanders.* (See page 144.)

PHIL ESPOSITO

ACTIVE YEARS 1963–1981

HIGHLIGHTS Art Ross Trophy winner* (1968/69, 1970/71, 1971/72, 1973/74), Hart Trophy winner† (1968/69, 1973/74), First All-Star Team (1968/69, 1973/74), Second All-Star Team (1967/68, 1974/75), scored 76 goals in one regular season (1970/71); *Hockey Hall of Fame* (1984)

In a land where toddlers strap on skates, Phil Esposito, a native of Sault Ste. Marie, Ontario, didn't discover hockey until he was almost in his teens. But he soon made up for lost time, relying on power, drive, and an eye for the goal to compensate for his lack of skating excellence.

After two years in the minors, he entered the NHL in 1963 as a center for the Chicago Black Hawks. Four years later, in a highly publicized trade, the rising star was sent to Boston where, in his second season, he became the first pro player in NHL history to score more than 100 points in a single year. In fact, he shattered the record with 126, earning for himself the first of five Art Ross Trophies as the league's leading scorer. In 1970, the hard-shooting Espo, together with junior teammate Bobby Orr, helped the Bruins to sweep past St. Louis in four straight games and bring the Stanley Cup to Boston for the first time since 1941. Two years later the championship flag again hung from the rafters of the Boston Garden, thanks largely to Number 7.

*Leading scorer   † MVP

He spent eight impressive years with the Bruins. In five of them—from 1970/71 to 1974/75—he scored at least 55 goals a season. He was twice voted MVP and twice awarded the Pearson Trophy by his peers as most valuable player. He was also named to the First All-Star Team every season from 1968/69 to 1973/74.

During the 1975/76 season, Espo was traded to the New York Rangers and, after four years, he retired at age 38, in a ceremony at Madison Square Garden. He left behind a career total of 1,590 points and 717 goals—a record exceeded only by that of Gordie Howe—and a single-season high of 76 goals, which has only been surpassed by Wayne Greztky.

After five years in retirement, Esposito returned to the NHL in July 1986 when he was named vice-president and general manager of the New York Rangers.

WAYNE GRETZKY

ACTIVE YEARS 1978–

HIGHLIGHTS Art Ross Trophy winner*
(1980/81–1987/88), Hart Trophy winner†
(1979/80–1987/88), First All-Star Team
(1980/81–1986/87), Second All-Star Team
(1979/80, 1987/88)

In his first nine seasons with the NHL, Wayne Gretzky has set more records than any other individual in league history. He is, in the opinion of many, the greatest ice hockey player of all time.

The oldest of five children, Gretzky was born in Brantford, Ontario, on January 26, 1961. At age 18, he joined the Edmonton Oilers, then a part of the World Hockey Association. In the following season, 1978/79, the franchise became part of the NHL and Gretzky scored his first league goal in the third game of the year. Since then he has compiled an astonishing NHL record. For example, he is the youngest player to reach 50 or more goals a season, the youngest to reach 100 or more goals a season, and the youngest to win the Hart Trophy for most valuable player. In total, he has amassed 629 goals in nine years of play. If he stays healthy, he may well exceed the record of his boyhood idol, Gordie Howe, whose 801 goals were acquired over 26 more seasons.

In addition to his personal records, Gretzky led the Oilers to the Stanley Cup finals six times and brought home the trophy in all but two of those years. His postseason total, 183 points, is the highest in NHL history.

Part of Gretzky's unique stature within the league lies in his almost European style of play. He brings to the ice a finesse that stands in marked contrast to the bruising style which prevailed when he entered the NHL. He also has an uncanny ability for "finding" the puck, for sensing the flow of a game, and for anticipating his teammates' moves. As for scoring, few, if any, players, are his equal.

*Leading scorer   † MVP

Gretzky, the only hockey player ever selected as the *Sports Illustrated* "Man of the Year" and until recently Canada's most eligible bachelor, married actress Janet Jones on July 16, 1988. In anticipation of that event, the tearful 27-year-old idol announced, at the end of the 1987/88 season, his decision to play for the Los Angeles Kings. Not surprisingly, his defection to the United States created a furor that rang from one end of Canada to the other. But there were cheers in Los Angeles. In the first half of the 1988/89 season, attendance at the Forum increased by more than 35 percent.

In the opinion of many, Wayne Gretzky is simply the greatest ice hockey player of all time.

Gretzky scores in the 1987/88 Stanley Cup finals, his last series with the Oilers.

In 1988/89, Edmonton's superstar joined the Los Angeles Kings, a decision that created a furor in Canada but brought cheer to southern California.

GORDIE HOWE

ACTIVE YEARS 1946–1971, 1973–1980

HIGHLIGHTS (NHL) Art Ross Trophy winner* (1950/51, 1953/54, 1956/57, 1962/63), Hart Trophy winner† (1951/52, 1952/53, 1956/57, 19/57/58, 1959/60, 1962/63), First All-Star Team (1950/51, 1953/54, 1956/57, 1957/58, 1959/60, 1962/63, 1965/66, 1967/68, 1969/70), Second All-Star Team (1948/49, 1949/50, 1955/56, 1958/59, 1960/61, 1961/62, 1963/64, 1964/65, 1966/67); *Hockey Hall of Fame* (1972)

T he annals of sport hold a unique place for Gordie Howe, whose professional career spans 32 seasons and five decades, a feat no other hockey player has exceeded.

Howe was born in Floral, Saskatchewan, on March 31, 1928. At 19, he joined the Detroit Red Wings for the 1946/47 season. He remained in Motor City for 25 years, during which he led the team to the final round of play-offs 11 times and to four Stanley Cup championships.

In 1971, at age 43, he retired, already the player with the longest career in NHL history. But Howe wasn't satisfied. After two winters of discontented idleness, he came back to play seven more seasons. Six were in the newly-formed World Hockey Association with the Houston Aeros, where he formed an "all-Howe" line with his sons Mark and Marty. In his final season, 1979/80, he returned to the NHL with the newly admitted Hartford Whalers. Finally, he retired—at the remarkable age of 51!

To survive in the rugged world of pro hockey for even a tenth of Howe's career requires considerable durability. At 6 feet 4 inches and 205 pounds, the

*Leading scorer   † MVP

man they called "Power" and "Mr. Elbows" had that. But he also had speed, dexterity, and the ability to shoot from either side. In his wake stands a formidable string of accomplishments, including a record 1,767 games, a record 801 goals and 1,049 assists, and a record 21 All-Star games (including one in his last season), with 12 appearances on the First Team. Off the ice, he's a champion as well, as generous with the fans as he is with worthy causes.

In typical fashion, "Mr. Elbows," Gordie Howe, drives the puck across the ice with dexterity, speed, and determination.

(Opposite) After eight years in the WHA, Howe joined the Whalers in 1979/80, returning once again to the NHL, his home for 25 years.

BOBBY HULL

ACTIVE YEARS 1957–1980

HIGHLIGHTS Art Ross Trophy winner*
(1959/60, 1961/62, 1965/66), Hart Trophy
winner† (1964/65, 1965/66), First All-Star Team
(1959/60, 1961/62, 1963/64, 1969/70, 1971/72),
Second-All-Star Team (1962/63, 1970/71), Lady
Byng Trophy‡ (1964/65); *Hockey Hall of Fame*
(1983)

W hen he was not quite three, Robert Marvin Hull, Jr., found his first pair of skates under the Christmas tree in his family's farmhouse in Pointe Anne, Ontario, and by nightfall he could skate unaided. When he was five, he was playing hockey with boys twice his age. By the time he retired from professional play in 1980, he was generally considered the best left wing in ice hockey history.

In 1957, at age 18, the "Golden Jet" joined the Chicago Black Hawks. Three years later he helped bring the Stanley Cup to the Windy City for the first time since 1938, one year before he was born. During his 16 seasons with the team he was the league's leading scorer three times, MVP twice, and a member of the First All-Star Team ten times. In 1966, he became the first player in NHL history with two 50-goal seasons to his credit. The following year he scored more than 50 goals again!

In 1972 he shocked the sports world by joining the fledgling World Hockey Association's Winnipeg franchise, giving the new league a badly needed dose of credibility. In his first season with the Jets, he earned the league's MVP award, and two years later he scored an impressive 77 goals. In 1979/80 he returned to the NHL for one more season, this time with the Hartford Whalers.

Hull will long be remembered for his blond good looks and his kindness to the fans, but even more for his blinding speed on the ice—he was once clocked at more than 29 miles per hour—and for his incredible power. If he didn't invent the slap shot, he certainly made it his own.

*Leading scorer   †MVP   ‡For gentlemanly conduct

(Right) *Bobby Hull waits for the puck so that he can deliver a quick backhand to the net.*

(Far right) *On March 25, 1972, Hull, Number 9, scored his 600th goal in a game against the Bruins.*

GUY LaFLEUR

ACTIVE YEARS 1969–1985, 1988–

HIGHLIGHTS Art Ross Trophy winner*
(1975/76–1977/78), Hart Trophy winner†
(1967/77, 1977/78), First All-Star Team (1974/75,
1979/80); *Hockey Hall of Fame* (1988)

E ven before he reached the NHL,
Guy LaFleur made a name for
himself by scoring a record
209 points with the Quebec City junior
hockey team during the 1970/71 season.
The following year, he joined the Montreal Canadiens. In his 14 seasons with
the club, he more than lived up to expectations, scoring 518 goals with 728
assists.

Beginning in 1974/75, he put together
a streak of six consecutive 50-goal
seasons. A year later, he took home the
Art Ross Trophy as the league's leading
scorer, a position he maintained for
three years in succession. He also
helped the Canadiens dominate the
league in the mid-1970s as the team
garnered five Stanley Cup Championships, including four in a row
(1976–1979).

In his prime, LaFleur was the NHL's
most compelling player, with hard, driving shots, a brilliantly improvizational
pattern of attack, and superior speed.
(See photo, pages 134–135.) Named to
the First All-Star Team for six straight
years, the ''Flower'' became the youngest player in NHL history to score 400
career points. He was also the youngest
to score 1,000.

In 1985, at 34, he retired, and in 1988
he was elected to the Hockey Hall of
Fame. But before the year ended he
came out of retirement to join the New
York Rangers. Rusty from his three years
of idleness and faced with the gradual
diminution of his skills, the hero of the
Montreal Forum still manages to find
occasional flashes of brilliance in his
revitalized career at Madison Square
Garden.

*Leading scorer   †MVP

*Guy LaFleur skirts around his opponents' net
in an attempt to sneak the puck past the
goalie.*

BOBBY ORR

ACTIVE YEARS 1966–1979

HIGHLIGHTS Art Ross Trophy winner*
(1969/70, 1974/75), Hart Trophy winner†
(1969/70, 1971/72), First All-Star Team (1967/68,
1974/75), Second All-Star Team (1966/67),
James Norris Trophy‡ (1967/68, 1974/75),
Lester Patrick Trophy§ (1979); *Hockey Hall of
Fame* (1979)

E ight-time winner of the James
Norris Trophy for his outstanding contributions from behind
the blue line, Robert Gordon Orr was
without doubt the foremost defensive
player of his day.

The trail to the top began in 1948 at
Parry Sound, Ontario, a tiny lakeside
town that used its frozen waters in
winter as a community rink. Bobby, a
skating prodigy, was encouraged by his
understanding family to leave home as a
young teen in order to participate in a
faster junior league program 100 miles
away.

At 18, the earliest age of NHL eligibility, he joined the Boston Bruins as a key
factor in the plan to revitalize the moribund franchise. Named Rookie of the
Year that season, Orr made good his
promise four years later, by leading the
Bruins to two Stanley Cup championships in 1970 and 1972, earning, in the
process, the Conn Smythe Trophy as
MVP in each of those series.

Modest, unassuming, but quietly
assertive in combat, Orr was every
Bostonian's favorite "box next door."
He handled adulation well, developing a
maturity and poise off the ice that
matched his prowess in the rink.

Plagued by knee problems from the
outset of his professional career, he was
made a free agent in 1976 and he joined
the Black Hawks in Chicago. But the
glory days were at an end. A sixth knee
operation soon followed and, after

*Leading scorer   †MVP   ‡Leading defensive player
§Outstanding service to hockey in the United States

attempting a brief comeback at the
outset of the 1978/79 season, he retired
on November 8, 1978.

In his relatively brief career—12 NHL
seasons—Orr left an indelible impression on the sport. In his ability to move
the puck offensively—a skill that earned
him two Art Ross trophies as leading

scorer—he virtually defined the role of
the rearguard and firmly established the
concept of an offensive–defensive
player.

Never content with sitting back in his defensive role, Bobby Orr sprints up the ice after clearing the puck.

(Following page) Orr battles Don Kozak for a loose puck in the Bruins–Kings meeting, January 16, 1975.

MAURICE RICHARD

ACTIVE YEARS 1942–1960

HIGHLIGHTS Hart Trophy winner*
(1946/47), First All-Star Team (1944/45–1949/50,
1954/55, 1955/56), Second All-Star Team
(1943/44, 1950/51, 1953/54, 1956/57);
Hockey Hall of Fame (1961)

Joseph Henri Maurice Richard was born in Montreal on August 4, 1921. He grew up in the hockey-intense French section of that city, a place where perfection on the ice is held to be the norm. In his 18-year career with the Canadiens, he became his home town's greatest star and its most fiery competitor.

He joined the team in 1942/43. Although a left-handed shooter, he was positioned at right wing, where he became part of a trio known as the "Punch Line" for its scoring proficiency. In his second year, the team lost only five games during the regular season, but dropped the play-off opener to Toronto. Then, in the second game at the Forum, after a scoreless first period, the "Rocket"—as Richard, a blazing skater, was called—scored three goals in one period, then added two more to make the final 5–0. By the end of the play-offs he had totaled 12 goals, still a record for Stanley Cup play.

The following year, 1944/45, saw Richard become the first player in the NHL to score 50 goals, which he did in a 50-game season. This record stood for 21 years until Bobby Hull, playing in 15 more games, reached 54 in 1965/66.

Despite his penchant for making goals, Richard never led the NHL in scoring. Being a left-hander on the right wing prevented him from earning the kind of assist totals needed for the Art Ross Trophy. The closest he came was in

1954/55, when a teammate, Boom Boom Geoffrion, edged him out by only a point. Perhaps he would have made it had he not been suspended during the last three games. Of course, that didn't stop the hot-tempered Richard, who was again suspended during the Stanley Cup play-offs, this time for pursuing an opponent who had drawn blood and for shaking off the official who tried to stop

him. The suspension, which infuriated Canadien fans, led to rioting in down-town Montreal on March 17, 1955, and resulted in $100,000 in damages

This mishap aside, Richard excelled in postseason play, earning a career total of 82 goals and 44 assists in 133 play-off games. He was also named to the All-Star Team 14 times in 18 seasons. Injury

ended his career at age 39. Usually a player must wait five years for election to the Hockey Hall of Fame. The way was cleared for the Rocket in nine months.

Maurice Richard proudly displays the puck with which he scored his 400th career goal on December 19, 1954.

OLYMPICS

NADIA COMANECI

ACTIVE YEARS 1973–1980

HIGHLIGHTS Olympic gold medal winner—women's all-around gymnastics, women's uneven parallel bars, women's balance beam (1976), Olympic silver medal winner—women's team gymnastics (1976), Olympic bronze medal winner—women's floor exercise (1976), Olympic gold medal winner—women's floor exercise, women's balance beam (1980), Olympic silver medal winner—women's all-around gymnastics, women's team gymnastics (1980)

At 4 feet 11 inches and 86 pounds, she did not look like a world-class athlete. But in the 1976 Olympic Games in Montreal, Nadia Comaneci, a 14-year-old girl from a mountain town in Romania, electrified the sports world with a series of stunning gymnastic feats.

On the first day of the Games, she shocked all onlookers by scoring a perfect 10 during the women's uneven parallel bars competition—the first perfect score in Olympic history. When the Russian contingent protested the scoring, Comaneci dismissed the controversy with the same bravado with which she approached the parallel bars. "I knew it was flawless," she said of her performance. "I have done it 15 times before."

During the next several days, she added six more perfect scores, three on the parallel bars and three on the balance beam. Her performance in Montreal netted her three gold medals, a silver, and a bronze.

Whatever the apparatus, Comaneci approached each competition similarly: she attacked it. During a parallel bars competition, an exercise lasting only about 20 seconds, she was a marvel of double twists and somersaults. On the balance beam, her best event, she delivered a stunning 90-second series of jumps, flips, and handstands.

But in October 1978, two years after her whirlwind Olympic performance, Nadia lost her world title. In 1979, rumors circulated that she was overweight and out of shape.

Then at the 1980 Olympics in Moscow, Comaneci, at 5 feet 3 inches and 106 pounds, won two gold and two silver medals, despite a slip on the parallel bars. At age 18, she held her own against younger, lighter competitors.

The onset of womanhood forces female gymnasts into retirement, so Comaneci's competitive life was indeed short, but she helped awaken the public to the world of gymnastics and left behind a magnificent record of achievement.

Nadia Comaneci, the 14-year old Romanian who dazzled the world at the 1976 Games, waves to the crowd in Montreal, a gold medal shining from her neck.

(Preceding pages) *Bob Mathias, the two-time decathalon champion, follows through on a discus toss at the 1952 Olympics in Helsinki.* (See page 155.)

(Opposite) *With a classic combination of grace and strength, Comaneci earns a perfect 10 to capture the gold medal on the balance beam at the 1976 Olympics.*

SONJA HENIE

ACTIVE YEARS 1923–1936

HIGHLIGHTS Olympic gold medal winner—women's figure skating (1928, 1932, 1936), world champion—women's figure skating (1927–1936)

C hampionship figure skaters have short careers. World competition begins when they are in their mid-teens, and retirement usually comes by age 20. Not so with Sonja Henie. Her reign over women's figure skating lasted 10 years and included three Olympiads.

She was born in Oslo, Norway, in 1912, the daughter of a shopkeeper who taught her to skate. At age 11, she won her country's national title, and a year later she competed at the Olympic Games at Chamonix.

Henie's Olympic debut was disappointing. She finished last in the figure skating competition, but she returned to Norway determined to become a champion. She studied ballet and integrated dance maneuvers into her skating routines, a tactic which no skater had tried before. The work paid off; she won her first world figure skating title in 1927.

Her next test was the 1928 Olympic Games in St. Moritz, Switzerland. There the 5-foot 2-inch, 109-pound world champion with brilliant blonde hair delighted the crowds. She performed like a ballerina on ice and won her first gold medal.

She retained her world title for the next four years and arrived at the 1932 Olympics at Lake Placid, New York, as the acknowledged queen of women's figure skating. During the Games, she won the admiration of the Americans and another gold medal.

After two Olympic championships, 19-year-old Henie still had no thoughts of retirement. She continued to compete and win world titles with one more goal in mind: a third gold medal at the 1936 Olympics at Garmisch-Partenkirchen, Germany.

In 1936, Henie encountered stiff competition. Cecilia Colledge of England, trailing Henie by only a few points after the compulsory program, gave an extraordinary performance in the free skating exhibition with a difficult routine that netted her a 5.7 rating in both perfor-mance and program difficulty. Henie had to be nearly perfect to win, and she was, executing a difficult routine flawlessly and bringing the crowd to its feet. She received two 5.8 ratings and won her third gold medal.

Henie turned pro after the 1936 Games. She toured the United States with her ice show, which made figure skating popular and Henie rich. She then turned to the movies and became a top box-office attraction. After her movie career, she returned home to Norway, where she died in 1969.

With balletic precision, Sonja Henie performs the compulsory figure exercises at the 1936 Olympics in Garmisch-Partenkirchen.

Following her Olympic career, Henie became a popular entertainer, with her own touring ice show, and eleven 20th Century–Fox movies to her credit.

JEAN-CLAUDE KILLY

ACTIVE YEARS 1960–1968

HIGHLIGHTS World Cup winner (1966/67, 1967/68), Olympic gold medal winner—downhill skiing, slalom, and giant slalom (1968)

Today's alpine skiers are specialists. They focus on either the downhill or the slalom events, rarely both. That was not the case in 1968 when a Frenchman named Killy turned in a triple victory at the Grenoble Olympics.

A descendent of an Irish mercenary who fought for Napoleon, Jean-Claude Killy was raised in the ski resort of Val d'Isère and began skiing the French Alps at age three. In 1960, at age 16, he won the French juniors championship and earned a spot on the national ski team.

At the 1964 Olympics at Innsbruck, Killy performed without distinction, but by 1965 he was dominating European skiing. The following year, he won the World Cup, and ski enthusiasts began predicting a triple victory for the handsome Frenchman in front of his hometown fans in the 1968 Olympics at Grenoble.

The first event of the Games was the downhill, not Killy's best. His countryman, Guy Perillat, the first skier down the mountain, covered the two-mile course in 1:59.93. A dozen skiers followed, and Perillat's time still held.

Then Killy attacked the course and finished in 1:59.85—a narrow victory and his first gold medal.

That was the first time that people around the world had seen the French champion. What they saw was a daredevil who paid little attention to style. Flying recklessly down the mountain, his arms flailing and legs widespread, he reached speeds of 80 miles per hour. "I take all the risks. That's my secret," he told reporters.

In the giant slalom three days later, Killy skied to an easy victory, beating the silver medalist by more than two seconds. The pressure built for the slalom, the final alpine event.

The slalom race took place on the last day of the Grenoble Games. On that foggy Sunday afternoon, two skiers, Haakon Mjoen of Norway and Karl Schranz of Austria, logged faster times than Killy, but both were disqualified for missing gates during their second runs. The ruling on Schranz came two hours after the event. So Killy had his third gold medal, a feat last performed by Tony Sailer in 1956.

Killy retired from alpine competition after winning the 1967/68 World Cup to race automobiles and to use his fame, good looks, and engaging personality to land commercial endorsements. In an age of ski specialists, his feat is not likely to be duplicated.

At Grenoble in 1968, Jean-Claude Killy turned in three daredevil performances for three gold medals.

BOB MATHIAS

ACTIVE YEARS 1948–1952

HIGHLIGHTS United States decathlon champion (1948–1950, 1952), Olympic gold medal winner—decathlon (1948, 1952), Associated Press Athlete of the Year (1948), Sullivan Award winner (1948); *National Track and Field Hall of Fame* (1974)

The winner of the Olympic decathlon is often called the world's greatest athlete because the competition requires the speed of a sprinter, the strength of a discus thrower, and the endurance of a long-distance runner. Bob Mathias had these qualities, and he held the title of world's greatest athlete through two Olympiads.

In March 1948, Mathias was an unknown high school track competitor in Tulare, California. He was good in three events—hurdles, high jump, and discus—so his coach suggested that he consider competing in the decathlon with an eye toward the 1952 Olympics. Mathias had never held a javelin or pole vaulted, but he liked the idea and began training. He progressed at an astonishing rate. That summer he won the United States decathlon title; instead of waiting until the 1952 Olympics, he found himself representing his country a few months later at the 1948 Games in London.

The decathlon involves 10 events, five on the first day of competition and five on the second. After the first day in London, Mathias was in third place behind Enrique Kistenmacher of Argentina and Ignace Heinrich of France. On the morning of the second day, Kistenmacher told Mathias, "Mathematically, I have it figured out you can't beat me." Kistenmacher's mathematics failed him. After the hurdles and discus, Mathias's best events, the American was in first place. He added to his lead with solid performances in the pole vault and javelin, then completed 12 hours of

At the 1952 Olympics, Bob Mathias so dominated the decathlon that his score of 7,887 points was 912 points higher than that of his closest competitor.

competition at 11:00 P.M. with the 1500-meter run. The 17-year-old high schooler had won a gold medal.

After the Olympics, Mathias enrolled at Stanford and played football. As starting fullback at 6 feet 2 inches and 190 pounds, he helped Stanford to the 1951 Rose Bowl. In the crucial win over USC, the victory that gave Stanford its conference title, Mathias ripped off a 96-yard touchdown run.

But as the 1952 Olympics came near, Mathias forgot football and concentrated on the decathlon events. At the Helsinki Games, the heavily favored Mathias led an American sweep of the decathlon and broke his own record for total points. *(See photo, pages 148–149.)*

Mathias retired after the 1952 Games undefeated in decathlon competition. He was the youngest male athlete ever to win an Olympic gold medal and the only one to capture the decathlon in two consecutive Olympics. In 1961, he used his Olympic fame to win election to the U.S. House of Representatives from California.

JESSE OWENS

ACTIVE YEARS 1935–1936

HIGHLIGHTS Big Ten champion and world record holder—100 yards, 220 yards, broad jump (1935), Olympic gold medal winner—100 meters, 200 meters, broad jump, and 400-meter relay (1936), consultant to U.S. Olympic teams (1968, 1972); *National Track and Field Hall of Fame* (1974)

(Above) *Jesse Owens gained national prominence at the Big Ten Track and Field Championships, May 25, 1935, when he broke three world records and equaled another.*

At the 1936 Olympics in Berlin, Owens not only shatters two world records but also the Nazi theory of Aryan superiority, as he and his black teammates dominate Adolf Hitler's games.

Born in a small Alabama town in 1913, Jesse Owens gained lasting fame as the black American who showed the world the lie behind Hitler's claim of Aryan supremacy at the 1936 Olympics.

Owens's journey to Olympic gold began during the Depression, when his schoolboy achievements earned him a scholarship to Ohio State University. There he burst into national prominence at the Big Ten Track and Field Championships on May 25, 1935, when he broke three world records and equaled another. The next year he qualified for the 1936 Olympics in Berlin.

It was to become the "Nazi Olympics," with Adolf Hitler presiding over a show of Teutonic organization that ominously foreshadowed World War II.

By the time of Owens's first race, the crowds at the magnificent Olympic Stadium had grown accustomed to seeing Hitler fawn over the winning Aryan athletes. The Fuehrer simply looked the other way, however, when the black American won the 100-meter dash in 10.3 seconds, equaling the Olympic and world records. Snubbed or not, Jesse Owens went right on winning. He took the broad jump with a leap of 26 feet 5 inches, a new Olympic record, for his second gold medal. For his third, the 200-meter dash, he set another world and Olympic record with a time of 20.7 seconds. Finally, for his fourth, he ran the first leg of the 400-meter relay. The team finished the race in 39.8 seconds, an Olympic record that would stand for 20 years. And Owens, with four victories, topped Paavo Nurmi, the "Flying Finn," who had captured three gold medals in 1924.

Jesse Owens came home with an amateur's honors and a Depression-era living to make. To support himself and his wife, he ran against race horses and sprinted against baseball players. Eventually, his celebrity enabled him to become a Chicago disc jockey. Not a militant, he served best as a role model for upwardly bound blacks until his death in 1980.

WILMA RUDOLPH

ACTIVE YEARS 1957–1963

HIGHLIGHTS Olympic gold medal winner—100 meter dash, 200-meter dash, 400-meter relay (1960), Sullivan Award winner (1961); *National Track and Field Hall of Fame* (1974)

Wilma Rudolph was one of the century's most unlikely sports heroes. She was born in Tennessee in 1940, the 17th child in a family of 19. By age four, she had contracted both pneumonia and scarlet fever. At age eight, she could barely walk, and she used crutches until after her 11th birthday. Less than 10 years

At a preliminary heat for the women's 400-meter relay in Rome, Wilma Rudolph, running anchor, leads the team to a world record.

later, she was an Olympic champion, the fastest woman in the world.

Rudolph succeeded because of dogged determination and family support. Each week, for example, her mother drove her to a clinic 50 miles from home so that Wilma could undergo therapy for her weak legs. Her brothers and sisters administered the prescribed muscle massages. By the time she was a teenager, doctors believed Wilma would walk normally and maybe even run a bit, but Wilma had greater expectations.

She increased her workouts, and her muscles responded. At 16, she stood 5 feet 11 inches and weighed 130 pounds. She made her high school girls basketball team and averaged 30 points per game. She ran track, too. Her coach alerted athletic officials at Tennessee State University to his talented runner, and Rudolph enrolled at the college after high school graduation.

At Tennessee State, her reputation spread as one of the fastest collegiate runners in the country. Her friends called her "Skeeter," short for mosquito, because she buzzed from the starting line to the tape so quickly.

The world found out about this special athlete at the 1960 Olympic Games in Rome. Her first event was the

100-meter dash, her specialty. She stayed with the pack for half the race, then shifted gears and won, breaking the Olympic record by a half-second. In her next event, the 200-meter dash, she used her long stride to beat the field and set another Olympic record. Later in the week, in the 400-meter relay, she ran anchor and came from behind to lead the United States team, composed entirely of Tennessee State runners, to a gold medal, Rudolph's third. When French reporters carried her story, they called her "La Gazelle" because of her long, elegant strides.

After the Olympics, she returned to the States and competed in the Milrose Games and the New York Athletic Club Games, the top track and field events in the country. She retired in 1963 and spent the next 20 years raising four children and working in physical education and recreation programs around the country. In 1981, she founded the Wilma Rudolph Foundation, an Indianapolis-based organization that promotes amateur athletics.

Rudolph, who could barely walk as a child, proudly displays her three Olympic gold medals, September 8, 1960.

A smiling Mark Spitz displays a fistfull of gold medals. He won two more that aren't even pictured!

The 22-year-old Spitz completely dominated men's swimming at the 1972 Olympics, winning four individual events and serving on three gold-medal relay teams.

MARK SPITZ

ACTIVE YEARS 1967–1972

HIGHLIGHTS Olympic bronze medal winner—100-meter freestyle (1968), Olympic silver medal winner—100-meter butterfly (1968), Olympic gold medal winner—200- and 400-meter freestyle relays (1968, 1972), 200-meter butterfly (1972), 200-meter freestyle (1972), 100-meter butterfly (1972), 100-meter freestyle (1972), 400-meter medley relay (1972), Sullivan Award winner (1971)

Many people remember the glamour photos of Mark Spitz showing a handsome young man with a handful of gold medals. This image sometimes makes us forget that Spitz was a superbly conditioned athlete who dominated his sport as few others have.

He was born in 1950 and grew up in Hawaii and California, good places for a kid who liked to swim. After numerous schoolboy successes, he made the 1968 U.S. Olympic swim team. Observers predicted that he would win gold medals in six events. In fact, he won gold medals for two relays and a silver and bronze for individual events. That would have been an accomplishment for most athletes, but critics called Spitz a flop, saying that he had choked under pressure.

Back in the States, he enrolled at the University of Indiana and led the school's swim team to three straight NCAA championships. In the process, he set 28 world records. He was ready for the Munich Games in 1972.

The man who arrived in Munich was 6 feet tall, weighed 170 pounds, and had a perfectly sculpted body. But the secret to Spitz's success was a pair of long, powerful legs that enabled him to kick six inches deeper than other swimmers could.

At Munich, he disappointed no one. Within a week, he had won every individual and team swimming competition that he entered and had set several world records. His closest competition came in the 200-meter freestyle. He trailed teammate Steve Genter for most of the race but charged in the last 50 meters to win by less than a second. In the team competitions, the United States squad, led by Spitz, posted amazing four- and six-second wins. Spitz won seven gold medals in all—an achievement never before equaled in Olympic competition.

The 1972 Olympic Games ended in tragedy—the kidnapping and murder of Israel's athletes by Palestinian terrorists. Spitz, a Jew, was hustled home after the murders. Unfortunately, this tragedy and the frequently reproduced photos have sometimes made us forget one of the great athletic achievements of the century.

In a typical Munich performance, Spitz appears to be all alone as he cruises to victory in the 200-meter butterfly.

JIM THORPE

ACTIVE YEARS 1908–1929

HIGHLIGHTS Olympic gold medal—decathlon, pentathlon (1912), football All-American—3rd team (1908), 1st team (1911, 1912), voted "Greatest Athlete, First Half of 20th Century" by Associated Press (1950)

Jim Thorpe was not only an Olympic great—the only athlete to ever win both the decathlon and the pentathlon—he was also a first-rate baseball player and a triple-threat football star (runner, tackler, and dropkicker). He was, by vote of the Associated Press, the greatest all-around athlete of the first half century. The polls remain open on the second half, but he is still without a challenger for versatility.

James Francis Thorpe, part Indian on both his mother's and father's side, was born in a one-room Oklahoma cabin in 1888, one of twin boys. In 1907, "Bright Path"—as he was known in his tribe—enrolled at the Carlisle Indian School in Pennsylvania. Glenn "Pop" Warner, who was to become a famous coach, built his winning Carlisle football teams and track squads around Thorpe's varied skills. Football fame came first; he was selected as an All-American in 1908 and again in 1911 and 1912.

Between football seasons, Thorpe went to Sweden with the U.S. Olympic team in 1912 and swamped the pick of the world's athletes in the decathlon and pentathlon.

A year later his Olympic triumphs were voided because he had been paid $15 a week to play baseball for two summers in North Carolina. While it was common at the time for collegians to receive money from athletic competition, those who did so usually used aliases; Thorpe naively kept his own name. So his Olympic records were gone, but no one could erase the memory of Sweden's King Gustav congratulating Thorpe, calling him "the greatest athlete in the world."

In 1913, he turned to professional sports, playing five major-league baseball seasons and helping to establish professional football as player-coach of the Canton Bulldogs. He made his final appearance, at age 41, in a 1929 game between the Chicago Bears and their cross-town rivals, the Cardinals.

The easygoing Thorpe had a difficult time during the Depression. He drifted to California, where he became a movie extra. He also worked with a shovel for the WPA for $4 a day; in World War II he served with the Merchant Marine.

In 1953, at 64, he died of a heart attack. Finally, in 1982, the Amateur Athletic Union restored his amateur standing in the 1912 Olympics, thanks largely to his family's persistence. His prizes, which had been refused by the runner-up, were removed from a Swedish vault where they had been tarnishing for 70 years and were returned to the Thorpe household.

Called the "greatest football player of all time" by the legendary "Pop" Warner, Thorpe was named All-American in 1908, 1911, and 1912.

Jim Thorpe unleashes the javelin in a 1912 meet for Carlisle.

A year after losing his gold medals for playing baseball at $15 a week, Thorpe was a star with the New York Giants.

JOHNNY WEISSMULLER

ACTIVE YEARS 1921–1930

HIGHLIGHTS Amateur Athletic Union 50-yard freestyle champion (1921), unbeaten in 10 years (1921–1930), Olympic gold medal winner—100-meter freestyle (1924, 1928), 400-meter freestyle (1924), 800-meter freestyle relay (1924, 1928).

T oday he is fondly remembered as the boyish but heroic jungle man of the movies but, before Hollywood beckoned, he was the dominant swimmer of his age.

Peter John Weissmuller was born in Windbar, Pennsylvania, but learned to swim wearing children's water wings in Chicago's Lake Michigan. After a turbulent and abused childhood, he joined the prestigious Illinois Athletic Club where his revolutionary high-bodied way of swimming quickly took him to prominence in AAU competition. By age 18, the muscular 6-foot 3-inch freestyler was a national champion.

Johnny Weissmuller in July 1922, a month after breaking four world records in one swim meet.

Although he was the greatest swimmer of the first half of the century, Weissmuller is best known as Tarzan, a role he played in 19 movies.

Two years later, at the Paris Olympics in 1924, he earned gold medals in the 100-meter and 400-meter freestyle—with record-setting times—and in the 800-meter freestyle relay. He returned in the 1928 Olympics in Amsterdam, adding two more gold medals to his collection, in the 100-meter freestyle—with a new record time—and the 800-meter freestyle relay.

Finally, in 1930, with more than 50 national titles and 67 world championships to his credit, he retired from competition, becoming a celebrity-representative for BVD swimsuits. This arrangement led Weissmuller to Hollywood, where an MGM screen test earned him the role of Edgar Rice Burroughs's hero, Tarzan the Ape-Man. It was a part he was born for; he was handsome, could outswim crocodiles, looked good in a loin cloth, and could even swing on a vine. When he added his ear-piercing yodel, a new folk hero was born. Of course, he did not have to call upon great acting skills. For the stolid Ape-Man, "Me Tarzan, you Jane" was a big speech.

In all, Weissmuller made 19 Tarzan movies, his last in 1947. In the following decade, the somewhat overage and overweight ex-athlete played another wilderness hero, Jungle Jim. The yodel was gone, but he remained a cheerful and likeable screen presence.

Perhaps Hollywood was not really the right place for an easygoing fellow like Weissmuller. Money flowed through his hands like water; there were five marriages, alimony squabbles, and bad investments. But, there were also grandchildren, a comfortable final marriage, and happy years in Florida. When he died, in 1984, at 81, he was still famous although he had not starred in a movie in decades. Through endless television reruns, his face, his physique, and his oft-imitated cry lived on and on and on.

TENNIS

ARTHUR ASHE

ACTIVE YEARS 1963–1980

HIGHLIGHTS All-American—UCLA (1963—1965), NCAA singles champion (1965), U.S. Davis Cup team (1963–1970, 1975, 1976, 1978), U.S. Open singles champion (1968), Australian Open singles champion (1970), Wimbledon singles champion (1975), doubles champion (1971); *International Tennis Hall of Fame* (1985)

In 1975, Arthur Ashe defeats Jimmy Connors to become the first black man in history to win the Wimbledon championship.

Born in Richmond, Virginia, in 1943, Arthur Ashe emerged from the segregated South to become the first black world-class male player in tennis history.

He learned the game at the playground where his father worked as a caretaker, but because blacks could not compete in Richmond's schoolboy tournaments, he transferred to an integrated St. Louis high school, where he won the U.S. interscholastic championship. On a tennis scholarship to UCLA, he became a three-time All-American and captured the 1965 NCAA tennis title.

When Ashe graduated college in 1966, he was 6 feet 1 inch in height and a slender 150 pounds, but his serve was frightening. He hit ground strokes very hard too. Some fans complained that his matches were boring because his zooming shots either skipped past lunging opponents or missed the court, creating few long rallies.

Two championships stand out in this great career. The first came in 1968, when Ashe, playing as an amateur, won the first U.S. Open (the championship that had replaced the U.S. Nationals), beating Tom Okker in the finals, 14–12, 5–7, 6–3, 3–6, 6–3. The second followed in 1975, when Ashe, at nearly 32 years of age, upset the heavily favored Jimmy Connors in the Wimbledon finals and became the first black male player to win the British title.

(Preceding pages) Billie Jean King at Wimbledon, 1982. She holds a total of 20 All-England titles in singles, doubles, and mixed doubles. (See pages 182–183.)

While these victories linger in the mind, Ashe is probably proudest of his key roles in the U.S. Davis Cup wins of 1968, 1969, and 1970. Indeed, he is fondly remembered for two marathon matches: a 6–2, 15–13, 7–5 victory over Ilie Nastase in the 1969 challenge round and a 6–8, 10–12, 9–7, 13–11, 6–4 win over Christian Kuhnke in 1970, the longest match in Davis Cup history.

A heart attack in 1979 and subsequent bypass surgery forced Ashe into retirement, but he captained the winning American Davis Cup teams in 1981 and 1982, and he has published numerous articles about tennis and other topics. His three-volume *Hard Road to Glory*, published in 1988, is a significant study of African-American athletes.

BJORN BORG

ACTIVE YEARS 1973–1983

HIGHLIGHTS French Open singles champion (1974, 1975, 1978–1981), five straight Wimbledon singles championships (1976–1980), ranked number one in world (1979 and 1980); *International Tennis Hall of Fame* (1987)

D espite his relatively early retirement, some tennis fans would argue that Bjorn Borg was the best there ever was—better even than Bill Tilden and Don Budge—and anyone who looks at his record would find that difficult to dispute.

He was born in Sodertalje, Sweden, in 1956 and began playing tennis at age 9. By 16, he was ranked number one in his country; that same year, 1972, he won the juniors title at Wimbledon.

In 1974, Borg, still a teenager, won his first major title, the French Open. A year later he successfully defended his French title and led Sweden to a Davis Cup victory as well. In the late 1970s and early 1980s, he won the French Open four more times, for a total of six, thereby breaking the record of four-time champ Henri Cochet.

But Borg's greatest triumphs came at Wimbledon. Beginning in 1976, Borg captured the All-England title five consecutive times, an unprecedented feat, and in the process won 41 straight Wimbledon matches.

The shaggy-haired Swede was an extraordinarily consistent player. He mastered all the strokes—the serve that always hit the box, the deadly accurate forehand, the hard two-handed backhand—but what made him a champion was his steadiness and composure. It was this quality that allowed him to get the best of his two great but volatile contemporaries, John McEnroe and Jimmy Connors.

In 1979, Bjorn Borg scores his fourth straight Wimbledon singles victory by defeating Roscoe Tanner in the finals.

The Borg–McEnroe–Connors matches reminded older fans of the great Bill Tilden–Bill Johnston battles of the 1920s. A case in point is the 1980 Wimbledon final, in which Borg lost the first set 1–6 to McEnroe, came back to win the next two, only to lose the fourth set after an endless 18–16 tie-breaker that would have shattered most players. Borg maintained his composure, however, and won the final set 8–6.

After a loss to McEnroe at the U.S. Open in 1980 and another in his quest for a sixth straight Wimbledon title in 1981, Borg lost interest in championship tennis and took a sabbatical. In 1983, at age 26, he retired.

The question of how good he could have been had he continued is moot. Bjorn Borg ranks with the best who played the game.

At the U.S. Open in 1981, Borg lost in the finals to John McEnroe. Surprisingly, the Swedish champion never won the singles title at Forest Hills.

(Right) *An extraordinarily consistent player, Borg's serve invariably hit the box. He also had a deadly accurate forehand and a hard two-handed backhand.*

DON BUDGE

ACTIVE YEARS 1934–1945

HIGHLIGHTS U.S. Davis Cup team (1935–1938), French National singles champion (1938), Australian National singles champion (1938), U.S. National singles champion (1937, 1938), doubles champion (1936, 1938), Wimbledon singles, doubles, mixed doubles champion (1937, 1938), first to win Grand Slam of tennis (1938), Sullivan Award (1937), Associated Press Athlete of the Year (1937, 1938), ranked number one in world (1936–1938); *International Tennis Hall of Fame* (1968)

After the great Bill Tilden lost his number one ranking in 1926, tennis was dominated for a decade by France's Four Musketeers and England's Fred Perry. In 1935, however, another great American champion arrived on the courts and ruled the tennis world with an authority unmatched even by Tilden

Don Budge, born in Oakland, California, in 1915, enjoyed many sports as a boy, baseball being his favorite. His older brother Lloyd finally convinced him to try tennis, and he mastered it quickly. He won juniors tournaments all over northern California and, in 1933, beat Gene Mako, his future doubles partner, in the national juniors championship.

In 1935, the 6-foot 3-inch redhead made the U.S. Davis Cup team and was ready for the big time. Though he had a fine serve and smooth, powerful forehand, his greatest weapon was his backhand, a stroke that he developed as a left-handed hitter in baseball.

Two years later, in 1937, he won both Wimbledon and the U.S. Nationals, but he is best remembered for the interzone Davis Cup rubber match that year against Germany's Gottfried von Cramm. Budge lost the first two sets, 6–8, 5–7, but took the next two, 6–4, 6–2. In the deciding set, von Cramm led 4–1, but Budge came on with a series of splendid strokes to tie and then beat the German, 8–6. When the game-ending forehand skipped past von Cramm, Budge was lying on the ground. The U.S. team went on to win its first David Cup in a decade.

Somehow in 1938 Budge topped his previous year's performance by becoming the first tennis player to win the Grand Slam: the Australian, French, and U.S. Nationals and Wimbledon. Late that year, he turned pro, which eliminated him from competition in the world's most prestigious tournaments.

In a 1970 poll, Don Budge, a man of high principles and a perfect sportsman, was voted the Greatest Living Player in the History of Tennis.

(Opposite) *In 1938, when this photo was taken, Don Budge had his best year ever. He won the Grand Slam and was named Athlete of the Year by the Associated Press.*

(Left) *On September 24, 1938, Budge defeated Gene Mako in the U.S. Nationals singles finals to complete the final step on his road to the Grand Slam.*

JIMMY CONNORS

ACTIVE YEARS 1971–

HIGHLIGHTS Intercollegiate singles champion (1971), U.S. Open singles champion (1974, 1976, 1978, 1982, 1983) and doubles champion (1973), Wimbledon singles champion (1974, 1982), ranked number one in the United States and the world (1976), in the world (1978), Davis Cup team (1976, 1981), World Cup Team (1976)

When Jimmy Connors was a teenager, his mother, a tennis-teaching pro herself, moved her family from St. Louis to southern California, the Mecca of would-be tennis stars, so that her son could have better teaching and tougher competition. The move paid off. In 1971, Jimmy, a UCLA freshman, won the National Collegiate Championship and then headed off on the professional tour.

At 5 feet 10 inches and 155 prematch pounds, the floppy-haired, baby-faced Connors is small among the lithe, hard-hitting pros, but he combines indefatigable baseline volleying with daredevil dashes to the net. His style, which also includes a two-fisted backhand and an unyielding determination to win, brought him five singles titles in the U.S. Open and two at Wimbledon. Together with fellow lefty John McEnroe, Connors dominated American tennis for nearly a decade, from 1974 to 1983.

Jimmy was also paired in the public mind with Chris Evert, two years younger, who emerged concurrently with Connors as the women's champion. Until each went off on his or her own "pro tour tangent" by marrying outside the mainstream of competitive tennis, the tabloids maintained a steady stream of Chrissy–Jimmy stories. In fact, these were more a matter of romantic speculation than hard-core truth.

Connors was last ranked number one in America in 1983. A year later he stopped winning. Curiously the player who captured a record 105 tournaments lost 54 in a row! It wasn't until 1988 that he took home a trophy again. It was the Sovray Bank Classic in Washington, D.C., not one of the championship cups he had won in his prime perhaps, but it broke the drought. Immediately thereafter he made his first competitive trip to France and won the $290,000 Olympic Open at Toulouse.

Jimmy Connors is no longer top-seeded in tournaments, but every fuzzy-cheeked teenager seeking center court status has to get past him. Connors turns most of them back, not with a veteran's guile, but with the same tireless persistence and driving shots that have always been his game.

(Opposite) *In 1982, Jimmy Connors won his fourth U.S. Open singles championship, defeating Ivan Lendl in the finals.*

(Left) *At Wimbledon in 1974, 22-year-old Connors displays the determination and two-fisted backhand that won him the men's singles championship over Australia's Ken Rosewall.*

MARGARET COURT

ACTIVE YEARS 1959–1977

HIGHLIGHTS Australian National/Australian Open singles champion (1960–1966, 1969–1971, 1973), French National/French Open singles champion (1962, 1964, 1969, 1970, 1973), U.S. National/U.S. Open singles champion (1962, 1965, 1968–1970), Wimbledon singles champion (1963, 1965, 1970), ranked number one in the world seven times, won Grand Slam of tennis (1970); *International Tennis Hall of Fame* (1979)

Her critics claimed that she suffered from center-court jitters, but Margaret Smith Court won more major titles in her long career than any player in tennis history. She played equally well at singles, doubles, and mixed doubles and left behind a string of championships that will never be matched.

She was born in Albury, New South Wales, Australia, in 1942 and quit school at age 15 to concentrate on tennis, which she first played with a piece of wood, the only racket she could afford. In 1960, she became a national hero when she won the Australian singles title, the first of 11 victories in her homeland's championship.

When she earned enough money to travel abroad, she competed in tournaments in Europe and America. Within three years, she had won all the major titles.

Like Althea Gibson, Court was tall—5 feet 9 inches—and she used her long reach to master the serve-and-volley game. She was also very fast; she was once asked to represent her country at the Olympics in the 400- and 800-meter dashes, but she would not interrupt her tennis career. Her training regimen, which included sprints and rigorous exercise, gave her yet another advantage over her female opponents: great strength and stamina.

Court's greatest tennis achievement came in 1970, when she won the Grand Slam—the Australian and French Nationals, Wimbledon, and the U.S. Open. (The previous year, only a Wimbledon loss had stopped her.) In the Wimbledon final, she played with a sprained ankle but outlasted Billie Jean King, 14–12, 11–9, in a match that seemed to never end. Compared to that marathon, the victory over Rosemary Casals in the U.S. Open final, 6–2, 2–6, 6–1, was a cakewalk. The victory made Court the second woman in tennis history to win the Grand Slam. That year, she also won the U.S. Open doubles and mixed doubles titles.

Today Margaret Court is known as Australia's greatest female tennis player. Her list of major titles suggests that she might be more than that—arguably the game's greatest female player.

Margaret Court shows reporters her Wimbledon Trophy, July 6, 1970. When she took the U.S. Open two months later, she became the second woman ever to win the Grand Slam.

CHRIS EVERT

ACTIVE YEARS 1971–

HIGHLIGHTS Australian Open singles champion (1982, 1984), French Open singles champion (1974, 1975, 1979, 1980, 1983, 1985, 1986), doubles champion (1974, 1975), U.S. Open singles champion (1975–1978, 1980, 1982), Wimbledon singles champion (1974, 1976, 1981) and doubles champion (1976), ranked number one in the world five times

S ome tennis fans suggest that Chris Evert's greatest contribution to the game was pushing her rival, Martina Navratilova, into becoming the greatest woman player in tennis history. Although there is some truth to that notion, it should not blind us to Evert's own career as one of tennis's greatest women champions.

Evert, who was born in Fort Lauderdale, Florida, in 1954, learned the game from her father, a tennis instructor, and her mother, an excellent club player. Her parents did their job well: by age 16, Chris was entertaining the crowd at the 1971 U.S. Open with her smooth strokes and zesty play. Billie Jean King beat Evert in the semifinals of that tournament, but observers knew that the youngster had the mark of a champion.

In 1974, while still a teenager, Evert won a record 55 straight matches, her first major titles—the French Open and Wimbledon—and was on the verge of becoming the top-ranked female player. She had smooth, easy ground strokes, a splendid two-fisted backhand, and above all the ability to concentrate intensely on every single stroke. She simply refused to make a bad shot.

With her first French Open and Wimbledon victories, Evert began a 13-year string during which she won at least one of the four major championships each year, including six U.S. Opens.

But certainly her confrontations with Navratilova are the highlight of her career. Evert beat her younger opponent

Chris Evert's intense concentration paid off at the 1978 U.S. Open, where she defeated Pam Shriver to earn her fourth Open championship in a row.

in 20 of their first 25 matches, and they played almost evenly through the next 20, but in the last seven years Martina has had a definite edge. Since 1975, the champions have met 14 times in the final rounds of major championships— six times in 1984 and 1985. In the pro-

cess, they have raised women's tennis to new levels of excellence—and have become close friends.

Early in 1989, Evert announced that she would compete in only a select group of tournaments and then retire at the end of the year. Soon afterward, there will be a spot for Chris Evert in the International Tennis Hall of Fame.

(Following page) In 1984, Evert met Martina Navratilova in six championship finals. Here, at the U.S. Open, it is Navratilova who will take home the cup.

ALTHEA GIBSON

ACTIVE YEARS 1946–1960

HIGHLIGHTS French National singles and doubles champion (1956), U.S. National singles champion (1957, 1958), Wimbledon singles champion (1957, 1958) and doubles champion (1957), ranked number one in world (1957, 1958); *International Tennis Hall of Fame* (1971)

She was called the Jackie Robinson of tennis because she fought racial prejudice and financial hardship to reach the top of the tennis world. Like Robinson, she displayed that rare combination of fierce competitiveness and personal dignity that made her a hero on and off the court.

Althea Gibson was born on a South Carolina cotton farm in 1927 and raised in Harlem. As a teenager, she skipped school and spent evenings hanging around pool halls. But like other city kids, she enjoyed street sports, including basketball and stickball. A local musician saw her playing paddleball and suggested she try tennis. She quickly became proficient.

As word of Gibson's skill traveled through the streets of Harlem, she came to the attention of the Cosmopolitan Tennis Club, a center for the area's white-collar residents. The club sponsored her first in local tournaments and later in national tournaments, though racial barriers often prevented her from competing against the country's best young players.

In 1946 at the ATA Championship, she drew the attention of Dr. Hubert Easton of Wilmington, North Carolina, an avid fan, and he invited her to live in his home and work on her game. The Eastons enrolled her in high school and sponsored her in tournaments. She later attended Florida A&M, where she played tennis and men's softball.

By the time she reached college, Gibson was 5 feet 10 inches and 140 pounds, which enabled her to hit with a force unmatched by female rivals and to cover the whole court in a few long strides. She began entering national competitions that were open to blacks and building her reputation. In 1950, she became the first black player to compete in the U.S. Nationals.

During the next decade, Gibson honed her skills and developed into the best female player in the world. She won both Wimbledon and the U.S. Nationals in 1957 and 1958, losing only one set along the way, and earning, in both years, the world's number one ranking. In 1958, at age 31, she turned pro, which eliminated her from major tennis events.

Although Althea Gibson never liked playing the Jackie Robinson role—her hero was Sugar Ray Robinson—her career has inspired all those who must overcome substantial obstacles to achieve success.

Shortly after this match, the Kent All-Comers Championship, held June 15, 1957, the winner, Althea Gibson, became the first black Wimbledon champion in history.

STEFFI GRAF

ACTIVE YEARS 1982–

HIGHLIGHTS Olympic gold medal winner—women's tennis (1984, 1988), French Open singles champion (1987, 1988), Australian Open singles cahmpion (1988, 1989), U.S. Open singles champion (1988), Wimbledon singles champion (1988), Grand Slam winner (1988)

C an a teenager be included among the great players in tennis history? If she wins the Grand Slam, she certainly can—which is exactly what 19-year-old Steffi Graf did in 1988.

She was born in Mannheim, West Germany, in 1969, and her parents, accomplished semipro players, gave her a sawed-off wooden racket when she was only four. Her first court was the family living room; but when she began breaking lamps, she moved to the basement and eventually outdoors on regulation courts.

She developed quickly. Before she was 10, Graf's dad, Peter, realized his daughter's potential and quit his job to become her full-time coach. In two years, his prize pupil was winning junior tournaments all over Europe.

In 1982, at age 13, Graf turned pro, and within three years she was reaching the semifinals of Grand Slam tournaments and earning the respect of Martina Navratilova, Chris Evert, and other top-seeded players. In 1986, she recorded her first tour victories, beating both Evert and Navratilova en route to 24 straight match victories.

Graf's first major title was the 1987 French Open. Significantly, she upset Navratilova, the top female player, in the finals, 6–4, 4–6, 8–6. Martina beat Graf later that year at both Wimbledon and the U.S. Open, but the next year Steffi swept the field.

(Opposite) *Steffi Graf demonstrates her powerful serve at the U.S. Open, 1988.*

(Above) *As Graf nears the end of her quest for the Grand Slam, she defeats Nathalie Herreman of France in the U.S. Open quarter finals.*

In 1988, Graf beat Evert in the Australian Open final. Then came the French Open, which she won by demolishing Natalia Zvereva in only 32 minutes. At Wimbledon in the final, she faced Navratilova, who was looking to win the All-England title for the ninth time. Although Graf lost the first set, she won the next two, 6–2, 6–1, to take the championship. She completed her Grand Slam with a three-set victory over Gabriela Sabatini at the U.S. Open. Then she jumped a plane to Seoul and won an Olympic gold medal. She began 1989 by destroying the competition at the Australian Open.

The key to Graf's success is a blistering topspin forehand, perhaps the best in the history of women's tennis. She is a tireless worker who complements tennis workouts with running, lifting weights, and jumping rope. And although she is big—5 feet 9 inches and 130 pounds—she is one of the tour's fastest players.

"I think she can do pretty much anything," says Martina Navratilova of Steffi Graf. The rest of the women on the tour fear that Martina is right.

BILLIE JEAN KING

ACTIVE YEARS 1964–1985

HIGHLIGHTS Australian Open singles champion (1968), French Open singles and doubles champion (1972), Wimbledon singles champion (1966–1968, 1972, 1973, 1975), 20 Wimbledon titles in singles, doubles, and mixed doubles combined, U.S. National/U.S. Open singles champion (1967, 1971, 1972, 1974), ranked number one in world five times; *International Tennis Hall of Fame* (1987)

As a girl, Billie Jean Moffitt liked playing baseball and football with the neighborhood boys, but her mother complained that those sports were not laydlike. So, with mother's approval, Billie Jean turned to tennis.

In Long Beach, California, where she was born in 1943, Billie Jean could play tennis all year long, and she quickly fell in love with the game. She enjoyed watching top players like Pancho Gonzales, Jack Kramer, and Althea Gibson perform at the nearby Los Angeles Tennis Club. A friend introduced Billie Jean to Alice Marble, the 1939 Wimbleton champ, and Marble began working with Billie Jean to develop her game.

Billie Jean worked her way through the California juniors, schoolgirl, and college competitions and, in 1964, trained in Australia under the great coach, Mervyn Rose. By then, she was ready to take on the top women players.

From 1966 through 1975, Billie Jean King (she married in 1965) dominated Wimbledon, with six wins *(see photo, pages 166–167),* and the U.S. Open, with four. In her best year, 1972, only a loss in the Australian Open kept her from a Grand Slam.

Despite her many international titles, King is perhaps best remembered for her participation in a $100,000 winner-take-all match at the Houston Astrodome on September 20, 1973. Her opponent was Bobby Riggs, the 1939 men's Wimbeldon champ who had made a comeback by challenging and beating top women players like Margaret Court.

Against Riggs, King used the same weapons that had made her a champion: the serve and volley, the killing passing shot, the baseline lob. King won in straight sets, 6–4, 6–3, 6–3, and called the victory "the culmination of nineteen years of tennis."

King has been semiretired since 1985, but she remains one of sports' most respected citizens. Her fight for equality for women athletes, as well as her remarkable tennis achievements, have earned her great respect both on and off the court.

(Below) *Billie Jean King defeated Julie Anthony in straight sets at Wimbledon in 1975. In the finals, she beat Evonne Goolagong Cawley for her sixth and last Wimbledon singles title.*

(Opposite) *King is perhaps best known for her victory over Bobby Riggs in the $100,000 "Battle of the Sexes" at the Houston Astrodome, September 20, 1973.*

JOHN McENROE

ACTIVE YEARS 1979–

HIGHLIGHTS All-American—Stanford (1978), NCAA champion (1978), French Open mixed doubles champion (1977), Wimbledon singles champion (1981, 1983, 1984) and doubles champion (1979, 1981, 1983, 1984), U.S. Open singles champion (1979, 1980, 1981, 1984) and doubles champion (1979, 1981, 1983), ranked number one in the world (1981–1984).

They call him a brat, perhaps with good reason. He screams at linesmen, insults opponents, and antagonizes the crowd. His enemies call it childish behavior; his fans call it fierce competitiveness, a refusal to accept defeat. Either way, John McEnroe plays tennis better than all but a handful of men who have tried the game.

He was born in 1959 to tennis-playing American parents living in West Germany and was raised on Long Island, New York. As a youngster, he played tennis, soccer, and the guitar, but tennis earned him a scholarship to Stanford in 1976.

When the lefty with the big serve turned pro in 1978, Jimmy Connors and Bjorn Borg ruled the tennis world. During the next three years, McEnroe engaged each in memorable matches. Borg owned Wimbledon, but McEnroe always denied the Swede the U.S. Open title.

Mac's best year was 1981. In July, he took the Wimbledon title from Borg, the man who had won it five straight times. In September, he won his third straight U.S. Open, beating Borg again in the finals. And, in December, he capped the year by winning three points in the final round of the United States' Davis Cup victory over Argentina. At year's end, McEnroe was ranked number one in the world.

Borg stopped playing in 1982, and McEnroe filled the breach, maintaining his number one ranking for three more years. In 1983 and 1984, he won Wimbledon, and he won the U.S. Open in 1984 as well.

But that was his last major victory. A talented group of newcomers has caused him to slip in the rankings, as have fatherhood, suspensions for improper court behavior, and a 1986 sabbatical. Still, there are flashes of the old champion—such as his splendid 4–6, 15–13, 8–10, 6–2, 6–2 victory over Boris Becker in 1987 Davis Cup play. Since Mac only turns 30 in 1989, his many fans feel that a return to the top is not out of the question.

Number one ranked John McEnroe seems pleased with his U.S. Open victory in 1984.

The left-handed McEnroe hustles for a return at the 1981 U.S. Open, which he won over Bjorn Borg.

MARTINA NAVRATILOVA

ACTIVE YEARS 1973–

HIGHLIGHTS Forty-eight major titles in singles, doubles, and mixed doubles, Australian Open singles champion (1981, 1983, 1985), French Open singles champion (1982, 1984), U.S. Open singles champion (1983, 1984, 1986, 1987), Wimbledon singles champion (1978, 1979, 1982–1987), ranked number one in world seven times

When Martina Navratilova turned professional in 1975, Chris Evert, her idol, had just emerged as the ruler of women's tennis. Three years later, she inherited Evert's crown and began a 10-year reign marked by achievements unmatched in tennis history.

Navratilova was born in 1956 to a tennis-playing family in Prague, Czechoslovakia. Her grandmother had been the country's second-ranked player. As a child, Martina worked at the game and dreamed of playing the world's best. That dream came true in 1973, when she was allowed to visit the United States and compete in a tour of top amateurs and young professionals. That same year, she won the juniors championship at Wimbledon and upset Nancy Gunter, a ranked pro, in an early round at the French Open.

But in 1974, Navratilova returned to Prague dissatisfied with her game. She was overweight. Her size—5 feet 8 inches and 155 pounds—gave her left-hand stroke enormous power, but she was slow on the court. She worked hard to get in better shape—a program of exercise, weights, a better diet—and it worked. She shed 15 pounds, and her game improved.

The year 1975 was a turning point in her career. Martina turned professional, reached the finals at the Australian and French Opens, and defected to the United States, where government officials would not interfere with her touring schedule and her main goal: to become the world's best woman player

She achieved that objective in 1978 at Wimbledon with a final-round victory over Chris Evert, her doubles partner. Martina came back to win their rubber set, 7–5, after trailing, 2–4 and 4–5. This was the first of Martina's eight Wimbledon titles. No one has won more.

For the next 10 years Navratilova, whose approach to the game has been called Machiavellian, ruled women's tennis. Besides her Wimbledon victories, she has won the U.S. Open four times, the Australian three times, and the French twice. Although Steffi Graf's Grand Slam shut Martina out of a major title in 1988, the final chapters of this outstanding career have yet to be written.

(Below) *Over the last 10 years, Martina Navratilova has dominated women's tennis, earning eight Wimbledon titles, the U.S. Open four times, the Australian Open three times, and the French Open twice.*

(Opposite left and right) *At the 1988 U.S. Open, Navratilova loses in the finals to Steffi Graf but still displays incredible power and drive.*

Bill Tilden was rated the greatest tennis player of the first half of the century in a 1950 Associated Press poll.

BILL TILDEN

ACTIVE YEARS 1913–1945

HIGHLIGHTS U.S. National singles champion (1920–1925, 1929), doubles champion (1918, 1921–1923, 1927), and mixed doubles champion (1913, 1914, 1922, 1923), Wimbledon singles champion (1920, 1921, 1930), U.S. Davis Cup team (1920–1930), ranked number one in world (1920–1925); *International Tennis Hall of Fame* (1959)

Bill Tilden's life was marked by athletic triumph and personal tragedy. Though he died penniless and disgraced, few could deny that he was one of the century's greatest sportsmen.

He was born in Philadelphia in 1893, the fifth and last child of parents who had lost their first three children to a diphtheria epidemic before he and his older brother, Herbert, were born. Tragedy continued to visit the Tildens. By the time Bill was 22, his parents and Herbert were dead. Young Bill never recovered from these losses.

As an antidote to tragedy, Tilden turned to tennis. In 1915, no one would have tagged him as a future champion—he had once been cut from Penn's tennis team—but he worked hard at the game and improved rapidly. In 1918 and 1919, he reached the finals of the U.S. Nationals, only to be routed both times.

After his loss in 1919, he worked hard to improve. His serve was already a powerful weapon, and his forehand was almost as damaging. But he made dramatic strides with a tentative backhand that had hurt him in his final-round losses at the Nationals, and in 1920 he emerged as the world's best player.

For the next six years, Big Bill—he was only 6 feet 1 inch in height, but his long arms made him appear taller—ruled tennis, winning the U.S. Nationals six straight times and leading the United States to seven consecutive Davis Cup victories. He also won Wimbledon twice, becoming the first American to win the British title. In 1926, the younger players—René Lacoste and Henri Cochet of the Four Musketeers—caught up with him, but he won the U.S. Nationals again in 1929 and Wimbledon in 1930, at age 37.

The last years of Tilden's life were unhappy ones. In 1946. he was arrested and imprisoned for a sexual engagement with a 14-year-old boy. Although the tennis world had been aware of his sexual preferences, most of his friends turned from him after the arrest and, after almost a year behind bars, he spent his final years with no family, few friends, and almost no income. He had squandered his money on large hotel bills and on unsuccessful plays and films which he wrote and in which he acted. After his arrest, his coaching income declined, and he died in 1953, penniless.

But Tilden's final tragic years could not erase one of the greatest athletic careers of this century.

Looking at this photo of the 1925 U.S. Nationals, it is easy to see why Tilden was called "Big Bill."

INDEX

Page numbers in **boldface** refer to photographs.

Aaron, Henry 10, **10**, 19
Abdul-Jabbar, Kareem 40–41, **40–41**, 53
Alexander, Grover Cleveland 11, **11**
Ali, Muhammad 64–66, **64–66**, 72, 80–81
All-America Conference 95, 113
Amateur Athletic Union 156, 163, 165
American Basketball Association 51, 55
American Football League 85, 101
American Tennis Association Championship 179
Anderson, Donny 96
Anthony, Julie 182
Army Air Corps 118
Art Ross Trophy *1950–51, 1953–54, 1956–67, 1962–63* 140; *1959–60, 1961–62, 1965–66* 142; *1968–69, 1970–71, 1971–72, 1973–74, 1969–70, 1974–75* 145; *1975–76, 1977–78* 144; *1980–81, 1987–88* 137
Art Ross Trophy 147
Ashe, Arthur 168, **168**
Associated Press 163, 174
Atlanta Braves 10
Auerbach, Red 43, 48, 55, 58
Australian National (Tennis) 194–195
Australian Open *1960–66, 1969–71, 1973* 176; *1968* 182; *1970* 168; *1972* 182; *1975* 186; *1981, 1983, 1985* 186; *1982, 1984* 177; *1988, 1989* 180

Baltimore Bullets 49
Baltimore Colts 88, 90, 95, 101
Baltimore Orioles 33
Barnett, Dick 49
Barry, Dave **79**
Baseball Hall of Fame 10, 11, 15, 16, 19, 20, 21, 23, 25, 27, 29, 30, 33, 35, 37
Basketball Hall of Fame 42, 45, 48, 49, 52, 55, 56, 58, 61
Baugh, Sammy 84, **84**
Baylor, Elgin 42, **42**, 51, 61
Becker, Boris 184
Bell, Tommy 78
Bellamy, Walt 49
Benitez, Wilfred 72
Berbick, Trevor 64, 80
Berlin Crisis 42
Berra, Yogi 11, **11**, 23
Berry, Ray 114
Bing Crosby Open 128
Bird, Larry 43–44, **43–44**, 52, 53
Blanda, George 85, **85**, 97
Borg, Bjorn 169–171, **169–171**, 184–185
Boston Braves 20, 30, 33
Boston Bruins 136, 142, 145
Boston Celtics 40, 42, 43, 45, 48, 49, 52, 53, 55, 56, 58–59, 61
Boston Red Sox 12, 16, 29, 37

Braddock, Jim 74
Bradley, Bill 49
Bradshaw, Terry 86–87, **86–87**
Breadon, Sam 20
British Amateur 120
British Open 122
British Open *1930* 120; *1946* 128; *1953* 118; *1960–61* 126; *1966* 123–125; *1970* 123; *1975* 130; *1977* **130**; *1978* 123; *1980* 130; *1982* 130; *1983* 130
British Womens Amateur 133
Brockington, John **90**
Brodie, John 107
Brooklyn Dodgers 21, 25, 30
Brown, Jim 82–83, 88, **88–89**, 102, 106, 113
Brown, Paul 95
Bruno, Frank 80
Budge, Don 169, 173, **172–173**
Buffalo Bills 106
Bukick, Rudy 104
Burns, Tommy 71
Burroughs, Edgar Rice 165
Butkus, Dick 90, **90**

Canadian Open 126
Candlestick Park 25
Canton Bulldogs 163
Carlisle Indian School 162–163
Carpenter, Georges 67
Casals, Rosemary 176
Caspar, Bily 126
Chamberlain, Wilt 42, 45–47, **45–47**, 59, **59**, 61
Charles, Ezzard 74, **76–77**
Charles, Ray 72
Chicago Bears 84, 85, 90, 93, 94, 95, 97, 102, 104, 113
Chicago Blackhawks 136, 142, 145
Chicago Cardinals 86, 163
Chicago Cubs 11, 20, 77
Chicago Stags 48
Chicago White Sox 49
Cincinnati Bengals 97
Cincinnati Reds 31
Cincinnati Royals 56
Clark, Dwight 97
Clay, Cassius 64
Clemens, Roger 12–13, **12–13**
Cleveland Browns 88, 95
Cleveland Indians 29
Cobb, Ty 8–9, 14–15, **14–15**, 31, 35
Cochet, Henri 173, 189
Cockell, Don 77
Colledge, Cecilia 153
Colonial Golf Tournament 118, **118**
Comaneci, Nadia 150–151, **150–151**
Conerly, Charley 113
Conn, Billy 74
Conn Smyth Trophy 145
Connors, Jimmy 168, 169, 174–175, **174–175**
Cotton Bowl *1979* 97
Court, Margaret 176, **176**, 182
Cousy, Bob 48, **48**, 52
Cy Young Award 12–13, 20

Dallas Cowboys 86, 92, 96, 97, 107, 111, 114
D'Amato, Cus 80
Davis, Anthony 108
Davis Cup 169, 189
DeBusschere, Dave 49, **49**
Dempsey, Jack 67–69, **67–69**, 79, **79**
Denver Broncos 85
Denver Nuggets 51
Detroit Pistons 49
Detroit Red Wings 140
Detroit Tigers 15
Devine, Dan 97
Dickerson, Eric 91, **91**
Didrikson-Zaharias, Babe **5**, 132–133, **132–133**
DiMaggio, Joe 16–17, **16–17**, 19, 23, 31, 37
Ditka, Mike 92, **92**
Downing, Al 10
Doyle, Jimmy 78
Duran, Roberto 72

Ebbets Field 27
Edmonton Oilers 137–139
Ellis, Jimmy 64
Erving, Julius 50–51, **50–51**
Esposito, Phil **136**
Evert, Chris 174, 177–178, **177–178**, 180

Feathers, Beattie 97
Fenway Park 37
Firpo, Luis 67
Folley, Zora 64
Ford, Whitey 21, 23
Foreman, George 64
Frazier, Joe 64, 65, **65**, 66
Frazier, Walt 49, **52**
French Nationals (Tennis) 173, 179
French Open (Golf) 122
French Open (Tennis) *1962, 1964, 1969, 1970, 1973* 176; *1972, 182; *1973* 186; *1974, 1975, 1978–81* 169; *1974–75, 1979–80, 1983, 1985–86* 177; *1975* 186–187; *1977* 184; *1982, 1984* 186; *1987, 1988* 180
Frisch, Frank 20

Garrett, Mike 106
Gehrig, Lou 18–19, **18–19**
Geoffrion, Boom-Boom 147
George Halas Trophy 90
Gibson, Althea 176, 179, **179**, 182
Gifford, Frank 106
Givens, Robin 80
Goalby, Bob 126
Golden Glove Award 25
Goldman, Charlie 77
Gonzales, Pancho 182
Goodrich, Gail 45
Goologong-Cawley, Evonne 182
Graf, Peter 180
Graf, Steffi 180–181, **180–181**, 86

Grange, Red 93–94, **93–94**, 97, 104
Grant, Bud 112
Greb, Harry 79
Green Bay Pakcers 90, 96, 107–109, 113
Greensboro Open 128
Greer, Hal 52
Gretsky, Wayne 136, 137–139, **137–139**
Groza, Lou 95, **95**
Gunter, Nancy 186

Hagan, Cliff 58
Hagler, Marvin **72–73**
Hairston, Happy 45–47
Halas, George 84, 97, 104
Harlem Globetrotters 45
Harmon, Mark 95
Harmon, Tom 95, **95**
Harris, Franco 88
Harrison, Bob 48
Hartford Whalers 140–141, 142
Hart Trophy *1946–47* 147; *1951–52, 1952–53, 1956–57, 1957–58, 1959–60, 1962–63* 140; *1964–65, 1965–66* 142; *1968–69* 136; *1969–70, 1971–72* 145; *1973–74* 136; *1976–77, 1977–78* 144; *1979–80, 1987–88* 137
Havlicek, John 52
Heeney, Tom 79
Heinrich, Ignace 155
Heinson, Tommy **59**
Heisman Trophy 95, 106, 110–111
Hemingway, Ernest 16
Henie, Sonja 152–153, **152–153**
Herreman, Nathalie 180
Hitler, Adolf 156
Hockey Hall of Fame 136, 140, 142, 144, 145, 147
Hogan, Ben 118–119, **118–119**, 123, 128
Holmes, Larry 64, 80
Holzman, Red 49
Hornsby, Rogers 20, **20**
Hornung, Paul 96, 107
Houston Oilers 85, 91
Houston Rockets 43
Howe, Gordie 136, 137, 140–141, **140–141**
Howe, Mark 140
Howe, Marty 140
Huff, Sam 90
Hull, Bobby 142–143, **142–143**

Illinois Athletic Club 165
Indianapolis Colts 91
International Tennis Hall of Fame 168, 169, 173, 176, 179, 182, 189

Jackson, Joe 15
Jackson, Reggie 10, 20, **20**
James Craig 91
James Norris Trophy *1967–68, 1974–75* 145
Jeannette, Joe 71
Jeffries, Jack 71
Johnson, Jack 70–71, **70–71**
Johnson, Magic 40, 51, 53–54, **53–54**

Johnston, Bill 169
Jones, Bobby 120–121, **120–121** 122, 123
Jones, Janet 137
Jordan, Michael 45, 51
Joyce, Don 84
Jurgensen, Sonny 107

Kansas City Chiefs 85, 107
Kansas City Royals 24
Kearns, Jack 67
Kellet, Don 114
Keltner, Ken 16
Kent All-Comers Championship **179**
Killey, Jean-Claude 154 **154**
King, Billie Jean **166-167**, 176, 177, 182–183
    182–183
King Gustav 163
Kitchel Stanley 71
Kistenmacher, Enrique 155
Knight, Bobby 43
Knox, Elyse 95
Komives, Howard 49
Koufax, Sandy 21, **21**
Kozak, Don 146
Kracken, Jack 75
Kramer, Jack 182
Kramer, Jerry 96, **96**
Kuharich, Joe 92
Kuhnke, Christian 168

Lacoste, Rene 189
Lady Bing Trophy *1964-65* 142
LaFleur, Guy **134-135** 144, **144**
LaMonica, Daryle 85
LaMotta, Jake 78
Lander, Polly 79
Landis, Kinesaw Mountain 20
Landry, Tom 92
Langford, Sam 71
Lapchick, Joe 55
Larsen, Don 11
La Starza, Roland 77
Leonard, Sugar Ray 72–73, **72–73**
Lester Patrick Trophy (1979) 145
Levinsky, Battling 79
Liston, Sonny 64
Lombardi, Vince 96, 107
Los Angeles Kings 137–139, 146
Los Angeles Lakers 40–41, 42, 45, 49, 51, 53–54,
    58, 59, 61
Los Angeles Open 128
Los Angeles Rams 91, 95, 112
Louis, Joe 71, 74–75, **74–75**, 80
Lucas, Jerry 52

Madison Square Garden 64
Mako, Gene 172
Malone, Moses 51
Mantle, Mickey 11, 22–23, **22–23**, 24, 25
Marble, Alice 182
Marciano, Rocky **62–63**, 74, 76–77, **76–77**, 80
Marino, Dan 97

Maris, Roger 24, **24**, 34
Martin, Billy 20, 23
Masters Tournament 121, 122
Masters Tournament *1937* 122; *1942* 122; *1949*
    128; *1951* 110; *1952* 128; *1953* 118; *1954* 128;
    1958 126–127, *1960* 126; *1961* 126; *1962*
    126–127, **126–127**; *1963* 123; *1964* 126; *1965*
    126; *1966* 123; *1967* 118; *1968* 126–127,
    126–127; *1972* 123, 128–129, **128–129**; *1975*
    123; *1977* 130–131; *1978* 128–129, **128–129**;
    1981 130–131; *1986* 123–125, **123**
Mathewson, Christy 11
Mathias, Bob **148-149**, 155, **155**
Maxim, Joey 78
Mays, Willie 25–26, **25–26**
McAdoo, Bob 40
McCauley, Ed 58
McEnroe, John 170, 174, 184–185, **184–185**
McGraw, John 20
Merchant Marine 163
Meyer, Ray 55
M.G.M. (Metro-Goldwyn-Mayer) 165
Miami Dolphins 97, 111
Mikan, George 55, **55**
Milrose Games 159
Milwaukee Braves 10
Milwaukee Bucks 38–39, 40, 56
Milwaukee Hawks 48
Minneapolis Lakers 42, 55, 61
Minnesota Twins 21
Minnesota Vikings 102, 111, 112
Mjoen, Haakon 154
Monroe, Earl 51
Monroe, Marilyn 16
Montana, Joe 97–98, **97–98**
Montreal Canadiens 134–135, 144, 147
Montreal Expos 30, 31
Moore, Archie 77
Most, Johnny 52
Munson, Thurman 20
Musial, Stan 27–28, **27–28**

Nagurski, Bronko 99, **99**
Namath, Joe 97, 100–101, **100–101**
Napoleon 154
Nastase, Ilie 168
National Basketball Association 40–41, 42, 43,
    45, 48, 49, 50–51, 52, 53, 55, 56, 58, 61
National Collegiate Athletic Association 40–41,
    42, 43, 52, 53, 56, 58, 61, 123, 161, 168
National Football League 84, 86, 88, 90, 92, 93,
    95, 96, 97, 98, 101, 104, 106, 107, 111, 112, 113,
    114–115
National Hockey League 134–135, 136, 137,
    140–141, 142, 144, 145, 147
National Track and Field Hall of Fame 155, 156,
    159
Navratilova, Martina 177–178, 180, 186–187,
    186–187
Nelson, Byron 122, **122**, 128, 130
Nelson, Ricky 97

New England Patriots 108
New York Athletic Club Games 159
New York Giants (Baseball) 20, 25, 164
New York Giants (Football) 89, 93, 112, 113,
    114–115
New York Jets 82–83, 100–101, 106
New York Knickerbockers 42, 45, 48, 49, 55, 61
New York Mets 10, 11, 25, 26
New York Nets 51
New York Rangers 136, 144
New York Times 20
New York Yankees 10, 11, 16, 19, 20, 23, 24
Nicklaus, Jack 123–125, **123–125**, 130
Nitschke, Ray 90
Nurmi, Paavo 156

Oakland Athletics 20
Oakland Open 128
Oakland Raiders 85, 96, 101, 107–108
Okker, Tom 168
Olympics *1912-Stockholm* 163; *1924-Chamonix*
    153; *1924-Paris* 165; *1928-St. Moritz* 153;
    1928-Amsterdam 165; *1932-Lake Placid* 153;
    1932-Los Angeles 5, **5**, 132–133, **132–133**
    1936-Garmish-Partenkirchen 152-53,
    152–153; *1936-Berlin* 156–157, **156–157**;
    1948-London 153; *1952-Helsinki* 148–149,
    148–149, 155, **155**; *1956-Melbourne* 58;
    1960-Rome 56, 61, 158–159, **158–159**;
    1964-Innsbruck 154; *1968-Grenoble* 154, **154**
    1968-Mexico City 161; *1972-Munich* 160–161,
    160–161; *1976-Montreal* 150–151, **150–151**;
    1980-Moscow 150; *1984-Los Angeles* 180;
    1988-Seoul 180
Orr, Bobby 136, 145–146, **145–146**
Owens, Jesse 156–157, **156–157**

Paige, Leroy "Satchel" 29, **29**
Palmer, Arnold **116–117**, 123, 126–127, **126–127**,
    130
Patterson, Floyd 64
Payton, Walter **2–3**, 88, 91, 102–103, **102–103**
Pearson, Drew 111
Pearson Trophy 136
Pender, Paul 78
Perillat, Guy 154
Perry, Fred 173
Philadelphia Athletics 15
Philadelphia Eagles 92
Philadelphia Phillies 11, 31
Philadelphia 76ers 45, 50–51, 52, 53
Philadelphia Warriors 45, 48
Pittsburgh Pirates 35
Pittsburgh Steelers 86–87, 106, 114
Player, Gary 126
Professional Football Hall of Fame 84, 85, 86,
    88, 90, 92, 93, 95, 97, 101, 104, 106, 107, 111,
    112, 113, 114

Professional Golfers Association Hall of
    Fame 118, 120, 122, 123, 126, 128, 133
Professional Golfers Association Tournament
    1940 122; *1942* 128; *1945* 122; *1946* 118; *1948*
    118, **118**, *1949* 128; *1951* 128; *1962* 123; *1971*
    123; *1973* 123; *1975* 123; *1980* 123
Pugh, Jethro 96

Quebec City Juniors 144

Reagan, Ronald 11
Reed, Willis 49
Rice, Grantland 97
Rice, Jerry 97
Richard, Maurice 147
Rickey, Branch 30
Riggs, Bobby 182, **183**
Riley, Pat 53–54
Robertson, Oscar **38–39**, 51, 56–57, **56–57**
Robinson, Bill "Bojangles" 78
Robinson, Jackie 29, 30, **30**, 179
Robinson, Sugar Ray 72, 78, **78**, 179
Rookie of the Year 25
Rooney, Art 86
Rose Bowl *1951* 155
Rose, Mervyn 182–183
Rose, Pete **8–9**, 31, **31**
Rosewall, Ken 175
Rudolph, Wilma 158–159, **158–159**
Russell, Bill 45–47, **47**, 48, 58–60, **58–60**
Ruth, Babe 10, 11, 19, 23, 24, **32–34**, 37

Saban, Lou 106
Sabatini, Gabriela 180
Sailer, Tony 154
St. Louis Cardinals 11, 20, 23, 24, 27
St. Louis Hawks 58–60
San Diego Chargers 85
San Francisco Forty-Niners 88, 97–98, 104, 106,
    113
San Francisco Giants 25
Sarazan, Gene 118, 132–133
Sauldsberry, Woody 59
Sayers, Gale 90, 104–105, **104–105**
Schmeling, Max 74, **75**
Schmidt, Joe 90
Schott, Marge 31
Schranz, Karl 154
Seattle Mariners 12
Seattle Supersonics 40–41
Sharkey, Jack 74
Shriver, Pam 177
Simon and Garfunkel 16
Simpson, O.J. **82–83**, 88, 91, 102, 106, **106**
Smith, James (Bonecrusher) 80–81
Snead, Sam 128–129, **128–129**
Snider, Duke 25
Southwest Amateur 122
Spinks, Leon 64
Spinks, Michael, 80

Spitz, Mark 160–161, **160–161**
Sports Illustrated 137
Stanley Cup 136, 137–139, 140, 142, 144, 145, 147
Starr Bart 96, 107–109, **107–109**
Staubach, Roger 110–111, **110–111**
Stenerud, Jan 95
Stewart, Bob 80
Sullivan Award 155, 159, 160, 173
Super Bowl *I (1967)* 107; *II (1968)* 96, **96**, 107–109, **107–109**; *III (1969)* 101, **101**; *V (1971)* 114, **114** *VI (1972)* 111; *VIII (1974)* 112; *IX (1975)* 86, 111; *X (1976)* 82–83, 102; *XI (1977)* 112; *XII (1978)* 111, **111**, *XIII (1979)* 86, **86**; *XIV (1980)* 86; *XVI (1982)* 97–98; *XIX (1985)* 97–98, **98**; *XX (1986)* 92, 102; *XXIII (1989)* 97–98, **97–98**
Swann, Lynn 86
Syracuse Nationals 48

Tanner, Roscoe 169
Tarkenton, Fran 112, **112**
Taylor, Estelle 67
Taylor, Jim 96, 107
Taylor, John 97
Tennessee State University 159
Terrell, Ernie 64
The Sporting News 43
Thomas, Pinklon 80
Thorpe, Jim 162–164, **162–164**
Tilden, Bill 169, 173, 188–189, **188–189**
Tittle, Y.A. 113

Tucker, Tony 80, **80**
Tunney, Gene 67, 79, **79**
Tunney, John 79
Twentieth-Century Fox 153
Tyson, Mike 80–81, **80–81**

Unitas, Johnny 97, 107, 112, 114–115, **114–115**
United States Amateur (Golf) *1916* 120; *1924* 120; *1925* 120; *1927* 120; *1928* 120; *1930* 120; *1959* 123; *1961* 123; *1954* 126
United States Davis Cup Team *1920–30* 189; *1935–38* 173; *1963–70, 1975, 1976, 1978* 168; *1976, 1981* 174; *1981–82* 168
United States Golf Association 133
United States House of Representatives 155
United States Nationals (Tennis) 173, **173**, 179, 188–189, **188–189**
United States Open (Golf) *1923* 120; *1926* 120; *1929* 120; *1930* 120; *1939* 122, 128; *1947* 128; *1948* 118; *1950* 118; *1951* 118; *1953* 118; *1955* 118; *1956* 118; *1960* 126; *1962* 123; *1966* 126; *1967* 123; *1972* 123; *1973* 130; *1980* 123; *1982* 130–131, **130–131**
United States Open (Tennis) *1962* 176; *1965* 176; *1967* 182; *1968* 168; *1969* 176; *1970* 176; *1971* 177, 182; *1972* 182; *1973* 174; *1974* 174, 182; *1975* 177–178; *1976* 174, 177–178; *1977* 177–178 *1978* 174, 177, **177**; *1979* 184; *1980* 169, 177, 184; *1981* 170, 184–185, **184–185**; *1982* 174, 176–178; *1983* 174, **174**, 184, 186; *1984* **178**, 184–185, 186; *1985* 186; *1987* 186; *1988* 180–181, **180–181**, 186–187

United States Ryder Team Cup *1937* 128; *1938* 128; *1947* 128; *1949* 128; *1951* 128; *1953* 128; *1955* 128; *1959* 128; *1961* 126; *1963* 126; *1965* 126; *1967* 126; *1971* 126; *1973* 126
U.S. Women's Amateur *1946* 133
U.S. Women's Open *1948* 133; *150* 133; *1954* 133

Vardon Memorial Trophy 128
Virginia Squires 51
Von Cramm, Gottfried 173

Wagner, Honus 35, **35**
Walcott, Jersey Joe **62–63**, 74, 77
Walker Cup *1922* 120–121; **120–121**
Walton, Bill 40
Warner, Glenn (Pop) 163
Washington Redskins 84, 97, 113
Washington Senators 23
Watson, Tom 122, 130–131, **130–131**
Weill, Al 77
Weissmuller, Johnny 165, **165**
Werblin, Sonny 101
West, Jerry **38–39** 42, 45, 61, **61**
White, Charles 106
Wilkins, Dominique 51
Willard, Jess 67, **68–69**, 70–71, **70–71**
Williams, Ted 36–37, **36–37**
Wilma Rudolph Foundation 158–159

Wimbledon *1920* 189; *1921* 189; *1930* 189; *1936* 173; *1937* 173; *1938* 173; *1939* 182; *1957* 179; *1958* 179; *1966* 182; *1967* 182; *1968* 182; *1970* 176; *1972* 182; *1973* 182; *1974* 174, 177; *1975* 168, **168**, 182–183, **182–183**; *1976* 169–171, 177–178; *1977* 169–171; *1978* 169–171, 186–187; *1979* 169, **169**, 184, 186; *1980* 169; *1981* 169, 177, 184–185; *1982* 166–167, 174–175, 186; *1983* 184, 186; *1984* 184–185, 186; *1985* 186; *1986* 186; *1987* 186; *1988* 180–181, 187
Winnepeg Jets 142
Women's World Golf Championship 132–133
Works Project Administration 163
World Cup (Skiing) *1966–67, 1967–68* 154
World Cup (Tennis) 174
World Hockey Association 137, 140–141, 142
World Series *1909* 35; *1927* 11; *1932* 33; *1936* 18, **18**; *1949* 16; *1953* 23, **23**; *1954* 25; *1957* 10; *1963* 21; *1965* 21, **21**; *1986* 130–131
World War II 95, 97, 122, 156, 163
Worthy, James 40

Zaharias, Babe Didrikson 6, 132–133, **132–133**
Zaharias, George 133
Zvereva, Natalia 180

PHOTO CREDITS